Dedication

This book is dedicated to all the men and women, who served our country in the past, and serve our country in the present and those who will serve it in the future. For those who returned and those who did not, telling their stories of honor, bravery, and sacrifice will preserve them for generations to come. Future generations will know that their freedom is not free, but rather paid for by the actions of those who answered the call to duty. World War II was won not only by the people in uniform, but also by whole communities in the allied countries that pulled together and supported the troops and the war effort. Therefore, this book is also dedicated to all who have supported our allied troops in times of war and peace.

The third group to whom this book is dedicated is the country doctors who put the needs of their community and patients first. Because they chose to serve alone in a rural area, they often served simultaneously as doctor, nurse, lab technician, surgeon, X-ray technician, and pharmacist, while also maintaining the medical records and billing department. They were a one-person show and did all for little pay, and sometimes received only commodities or even a trade of services. Those doctors deserve our deep gratitude for sacrificing time away from their families as they were on call around the clock.

Acknowledgements

My deepest gratitude to the following individuals for their contributions to this book:

Sincere thanks to Dave Allen, the president of the Scott Hosier Veterans Roundtable, (formerly known as the WWII Roundtable) in Rochester, Minnesota, for critiquing the historical content and general format.

My gratitude to Ellen Bisping for editing and writing her endorsement of the book. As both my former English teacher and a member of my church, she inspired my love of literature.

Special appreciation to my daughter Allison Cooney for reviewing the final draft.

I'm grateful to my sister, Brenda Eisenschenk, for sharing the poem she wrote and read at our grandfather's funeral.

Thank you to Julie Schrader of Minnesota Heritage Publishing for being so wonderful to work with in both editing the photos and guiding me in this journey.

I deeply appreciate the invaluable contributions of Betsy Sherman, the copy editor, and Michael Sellner, designer at Corporate Graphics, for his hard work with the layout and cover design.

Heartfelt thanks to Dave and Edna Thayer, and Susie Wright for their input and sharing memories.

A special thank you for her expert advice to Stefanie (Zehnder) Whitney, a teacher at Mayo High School in Rochester, Minnesota, who grew up in Truman, Minnesota, and whose family has been in the Truman area since 1951.

Introduction

Hearing the stories of World War II veterans is always fascinating for me. My grandfather rarely talked about his experiences in the war, so his story could have been one of the many untold from a great era. About seven years after my grandfather's death, my father opened a box he had inherited that contained my grandfather's uniform. My father wanted to give it to my son, who is now in the military. I was amazed at what we discovered underneath the uniform. The box held about 250 photos from the war, my grandfather's military journal, letters, medals, and an 8mm film of South Carolina and Tinian Island. I could not put the journal down until I had finished every word. It gave me a glimpse of my grandfather's experiences that no one in my family had been aware of before. A friend whom I told of the discovery asked me to talk to her history class at Century High School in Rochester, Minnesota. When I took the photos to the local Target store to scan them for the presentation, to my surprise, standing behind me in line was Tom Hosier of the Scott Hosier World War II Roundtable. He asked about the photos, told me about the World War II Roundtable, and encouraged me to attend its next monthly meeting and use it as a resource for my presentation. I have thoroughly enjoyed all the meetings I have attended since.

I asked my parents to give the school presentation with me giving each of us a different topic to highlight. My mother began the presentation to the class by talking about the war in Germany and the book she wrote, *Feisty Lydia*, about our neighbor who was a young girl in Germany during World War II and became a war bride. Dad described what it was like being in Junior High during the war and how the war had affected the family. Finally, I told the students about my grandfather's journal and showed the photos on PowerPoint while my father passed around mementos such as my grandfather's uniform, medals, and helmet.

After giving the presentation several times, I have been encouraged to share with you my grandfather's story. I have tried to preserve here his story as he recorded it through his photos and journal. To truly understand a person, one must look at his character and learn where those traits originated. To understand who Captain Mike Thayer was, we must return to the beginning…his beginning.

All actual heroes are essential men,
And all men possible heroes.

— *E.B. Browning*

TABLE OF CONTENTS

iii   Dedication

iv   Acknowledgements

v   Introduction

1   Chapter 1   A Purposeful Birth

11   Chapter 2   Childhood

15   Chapter 3   Becoming a Doctor

17   Chapter 4   Helen

21   Chapter 5   Starting a Family and Career

29   Chapter 6   Life as a Country Doctor

33   Chapter 7   Call to Duty

39   Chapter 8   Oakland, California

49   Chapter 9   Fort Jackson, South Carolina

57   Chapter 10   Tinian Island

99   Chapter 11   Fukuoka, Japan

143   Chapter 12   Continuing Practice After the War

153   Chapter 13   Blessings of Children, Grandchildren, and Great-grandchildren

163   Chapter 14   Community Involvement

169   Chapter 15   Keeping in Touch

173   Chapter 16   Effects of the War on a Country Doctor

179   Afterword: Author's Portrait of a Real Hero

181   Timeline

184   About the Author

Mike's Parents: Leroy and Maude Thayer

1

A Purposeful Birth

The life of a country doctor who would one day serve his country began on June 12, 1907, with Ellsworth "Mike" Thayer as a small bundle of joy in the arms of Maude Thayer. Maude and Leroy Thayer and their three children were a close Christian family living in Clarissa, Minnesota. The children were nicely spaced two and a half years apart. Maude was serving as the country superintendent of Sunday school for the Methodist church, and Leroy was a bank clerk. His hard work would eventually pay off, as he bought the bank in Clarissa and, later, one in North Dakota. Leroy had changed his birth name from David Leroy to Leroy David because he believed David was not a banker's name. After the change, people called him Roy, and he liked that, thinking it sounded more professional.

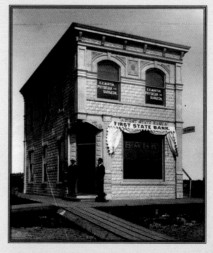

The First State Bank in Kensal, North Dakota that Leroy owned. Leroy "Roy" stands with his employee, Randal, around 1900.

Inside the Clarissa State Bank in Clarissa, Minnesota, ca. 1906. Left to right are a bank employee, Maude, and Leroy.

Clarissa State Bank, ca. 1906-1908.

The arrow on the right points down at Leroy's bank, the Clarissa State Bank. Leroy saved every penny and invested in three farms, which he rented to others. Life was good for this hardworking family until 10-year-old Blanch Vivian died of rheumatic fever on July 12, 1906. She was the middle child, and Maude was broken-hearted over her death. Family and friends from all over came to the viewing in the family's front parlor. Although Maude's heart was so broken over the death of her daughter, just a few months later her heart was filled with hope as she learned she was expecting again.

Downtown Clarissa, Minnesota.

On June 12, 1907, Maude went into labor, and knew she would be giving birth soon so Dr. Charles Ellsworth Reeves was called from Eagle Bend to Clarissa to deliver the baby. Maude had delivered all of her babies at home, and this one was to be no different. Maude and Leroy welcomed into the world a new baby boy. Now what to name him? They thought for a minute, and decided to name him Ellsworth after the doctor who helped bring him into the world and Albert after his grandfather, Albert Augustus Thayer. Ellsworth was born just eleven months after his sister's death. No one will ever know for sure whether his birth was an attempt to heal a broken heart, but restoring joy to his mother's life certainly gave him purpose.

Birthplace of Ellsworth Albert in Clarissa, Minnesota.

Ellsworth's Baptism.

Ellsworth at six months old. A relative owned a company in Minneapolis that made these Thayer baby carriages.

Ellsworth was born into a pioneer family that taught him the importance of serving the entire community. The hardships of his family and his ancestors would prove to Ellsworth that with determination, he could endure nearly anything. His grandfathers, William Cooper and Albert Augustus Thayer, were prominent men in their communities and proudly served their country during the Civil War.

Thayer family photo. Front row, left to right: Mary "Elizabeth," and Maude holding Ellsworth "Mike." Back row: William "Bill" and Leroy "Roy."

Ellsworth's maternal great-grandfather, James Cooper, was one of the first settlers in the Minnesota Territory. Born in 1805 in the County Cork, Ireland, he married Isabell Neill in 1831, and they had a daughter, Rachel. In 1832 she died at sea at eight months old, while the family was en route to America. Their second child, Sarah, was born in Canada. After James and Isabelle settled in Pennsylvania, John, William, Isabelle, Elizabeth, Margaret, and James were born. When Isabelle died in 1850 at 37, her youngest was three. James was now a single parent of seven children. James married Nancy Minard in 1853, and they had two children: Rocselana, born in 1853, and Roland, born in 1856.

James left Nancy alone to care for the nine children while he traveled west on horseback to find land to farmstead. He built a log home in the Minnesota Territory and started on the long journey back to Pennsylvania to get the family. While he was gone, Indians burned down the log house he had built. The Coopers traveled to Minnesota by covered wagon, with the sons riding horseback. When they arrived, they rebuilt their home and befriended the neighboring Indians. To help keep the peace, James invited Quakers to farm the surrounding lands. The tribe had many confrontations with the other white settlers in the area but none with the Coopers or the Quakers after they became friends.

James gave the biblical name Bethel to the town he helped to establish. He farmed and ran a stagecoach for passengers and mail delivery. Nancy taught school, first at home and then in a small schoolhouse built on the corner of their farm called Coopers School. As a store and other buildings arose around that corner, it became known as Coopers Corner.

Samuel, born in 1859, was the eleventh child of James and the first of the family to be born in Minnesota. James named two small neighboring lakes in Bethel, Cooper and Minard, the latter after his wife's maiden name. Nancy

Private William Cooper

William and Lizzie Cooper

died May 25, 1866 at 45. Two years later, in 1868, James married Rebecca Pauline Milligan, and they had three children: Evaline, Mary, and Laura.

William, the fourth child of James worked hard to build and support his community. When the Civil War began, both William and his older brother, John, served in the Union in the Minnesota Eighth Regiment, Company A. William was wounded in the Battle of the Cedars. Little of the Bethel population was left after the war since most of the pacifist Quakers had left. In 1865 William moved to Fair Haven Township as did his sister Isabelle (Cooper) Grinols and her husband, Benjamin. William worked as the Fair Haven postmaster and owned a merchandise store with Benjamin. William married Lizzie Noyes, and the two families were successful merchants in the area. William and his brother John donated the land on which St. Benedict College was built. William and Lizzie had three children: Minnie, Maude, and Blanche Cooper. Maude would become the wife of Leroy Thayer and the mother of Ellsworth. (Note that the township of Fair Haven is spelled as two words. Mr. Haven was the surveyor of the land for this new settlement and the people thought he was fair so they named it Fair Haven Township. It becomes one word when it is later incorporated as the city Fairhaven.)

Albert Augustus Thayer

Ellsworth's paternal grandfather was Albert Augustus Thayer, whom he called Grandpa Gus. Gus, a descendant of Capt. Miles Standish from the

Mayflower, was born in Adrian, Michigan. In 1854, when he was six his family moved out west to Osseo in the Minnesota Territory as some of the first settlers in that area. The neighboring Sioux were attacking settlers so as a teenager, Gus slept in the barn with a loaded rifle and a horse saddled at all times in case of an attack on his family. At 16, Gus fibbed about his age to serve as a drummer boy in Company C of the Minnesota Seventh Volunteer Infantry. After the war, he married Mary Colburn, a granddaughter of Civil War patriot Barbara Fritchie, and had two sons, William Warren and David Leroy. David Leroy was a year old when his mother died at 24. Gus operated the hotel in Fairhaven and one in Annandale; he also ran a stagecoach between the two cities, bringing customers from the train to the hotels. After Mary's death, Gus married Caroline Hill and had five more children.

When the hotel he was managing in Annandale burned down, the owners decided not to rebuild. However, the railroad liked how Gus had managed the former hotel and knew it was important for their business to have hotels at the train stops. The railroad officials loaned him the money to build the Thayer Hotel in the same location. Caroline, an excellent cook managed the upper class dining room. The train had the capacity to deliver oysters and sea food from the East coast which proved to be a favorite among her guests. The hotel became a favorite restaurant for both hotel guests and the neighboring community. Many train passengers were also served meals before continuing on from Annandale. Ellsworth's mother, Maude Thayer, often told her grandson, David, that it was a hard life working in the hotel. She especially disliked carrying a container of hot coals to put under each bed for warmth in the winter. The maids had a separate stairway to use to carry warm pitchers of water upstairs to fill the bathtubs. Gus entertained guests on the piano, and the hotel became a popular meeting and social gathering place. It hosted the meetings for the Grand Army of the Republic (GAR), the ladies' aid society, and other groups. GAR was founded in 1866 for men who served in the Union Army or Navy during the Civil War. Gus was a founder of the local GAR chapter in Annandale, Minnesota.

The J.L. Buzzell Post, of the Grand Army of the Republic in Annandale, Minnesota, in 1906. Left to right, first row, George Walters, Jake Lambert, Charles Bayliss, Alex Fashaut, and Charles Gille; second row, P.A. Rudolph, William Dorman, Ed Kemp, W.H. Towle, O.H. Miller, and Edwin Whitlock; third row, L.R. Niles, W. Webster, A.A. Thayer, Barney Lamson, William McBride, William Boutwell, and Adam Ringer.—Photo courtesy of Mrs. Rochat. (from the *Annandale Advocate*).

Ellsworth's grandparents and great-grandparents impressed upon him the importance of being active in the community and doing everything possible to help it thrive! He was proud that his grandparents were among the early pioneers who had helped to shape the Minnesota Territory into a great state.

In every conceivable manner, the family is a link to our past, a bridge to our future.
— *Alex Haley*

Mike about two years old with his red curly hair.

2

CHILDHOOD

A Nickname 'Mike'

The Thayer name is English, and Ellsworth is also English. Ellsworth had English, Irish, and Scottish ancestry from his father's side of the family, and Irish and English from his mother's side. By the time Ellsworth was two, his father noticed his red hair and ruddy complexion looked more Irish and gave him a nickname to match. "Mike" stuck with him for the rest of his life.

Mike about four years old.

Glimpses of Mike's Family Life as a Child

Mike looked up to his much older brother and sister. His brother, Bill, was in the ROTC and Mike decided he wanted to go into the military, too.

Mike's siblings had to ride horseback or use a horse and buggy to get to school each day. By the time Mike was in high school, the family had a car, which caused a bit of resentment for the older siblings. It was in 1912 that Henry Ford started the idea of an assembly line and was able to build the Model T Ford more efficiently making it readily available and more affordable.

Mike's father worked long hours in the bank and left much of the parenting to Maude. She was very religious and encouraged Mike in the Methodist faith. During those years of affluence, they were able to have a live-in maid from Sweden.

Mike raised a Shetland pony in town that he loved to ride. He joined the boys' club, which was the predecessor to the 4-H club. He acquired cattle to raise and entered them along with his horse in the county fair and won ribbons.

Standing: William Cooper Thayer, Mary "Elizabeth" Thayer
Sitting: Maude Thayer, Ellsworth Thayer, and Leroy Thayer

When Mike was a teenager, hard times befell the family. An average of 600 banks were closing every year. Mike's father had invested in the three farms which they rented to others during the years of prosperity between 1900 and 1920. However, in 1920, farm values fell sharply beginning a twenty year period of financial difficulty for most farmers. Many battled a plague of grasshoppers, Minnesota's extreme weather changes, and droughts. The families that managed to endure those conditions had to deal with the decreasing value of their farms. Many were unable to repay their bank loans and lost their farms to the bank. Struggling banks sold the farmland at a loss because the decrease in farm value made the total sale less than the original farm loan extended from the bank to the farmer. As a result, many banks closed as well. Mike's father lost both of his banks and all three of his farms. He drove Mike to the corner of a field and told him to make a choice. Leroy had made arrangements with the farmer to take Mike into his home and teach him the trade of farming. Maude wanted him to be either a doctor or a preacher. Although farming interested him, Mike did not think he could be a farmer or a preacher, so he prepared for medical school. Maude had strongly encouraged him to become a doctor and he was glad she had. The family sold their beautiful home and auctioned off most of their property in Clarissa. They moved from Clarissa to a house in south Minneapolis that Leroy and Maude rented from a landlord and they in turn sub-rented parts of it to others. Mike graduated from West High School in Minneapolis in 1925.

Ellsworth "Mike" Thayer's high school graduation photo 1925, West High School, Minneapolis, Minnesota.

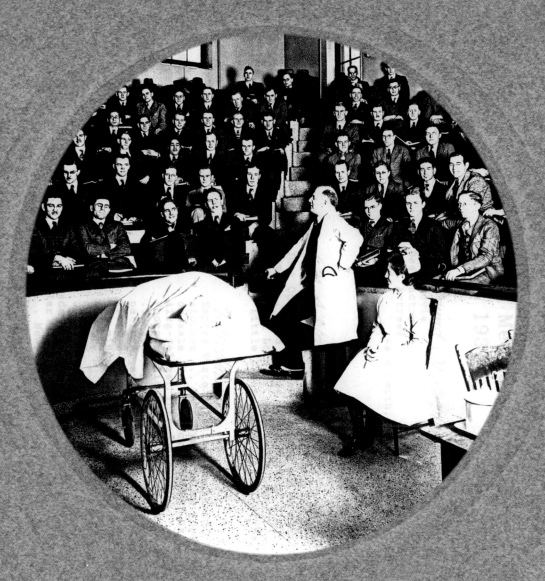

University of Minnesota medical school classroom. Mike is seated on the far right in the front row.

3

Becoming a Doctor

Mike lived at home at 2712 Bryant Avenue South in Minneapolis while going to college. He attended school during the day and worked in a drugstore in the evenings while attending medical school at the University of Minnesota Twin Cities campus. He was often so tired that Maude and his older sister, Elizabeth, would read aloud from the text books while Mike closed his eyes to rest. Elizabeth was fourteen years older and knew how important it was for him to finish medical school. Years later she would talk about how she helped him study.

On October 27, 1929, the New York Stock Market crashed, which became known as "Black Tuesday". This officially began The Great Depression. The 1929 stock market crash took what little Leroy Thayer had left. The 1930 Federal Census taken on April 9, shows that three lodgers were living in Leroy and Maude's household. After the boarders were taken in Mike had to share a room with his father and his sister shared a room with Maude. When it seemed as if things could get no worse, just seven days after the census was taken, Leroy died of a heart attack on April 16 at the age of 56. Was the stress of working so hard to provide a comfortable life for his family only to lose it all in just a few years too much to take? Mike was in the same bed with his father when he heard him take his last breath. Imagine how Mike felt. Even though Mike was in medical school, there was nothing he could do to save his father.

Helen about the time of their wedding.

4

HELEN

Mike met the love of his life while she was in training at St. Andrew's Hospital School of Nursing in Minneapolis. Helen Gallehue had seen equally hard times and shared Mike's love of medicine and the desire for a better life. Helen also knew what it was like to be born into a comfortable lifestyle only to lose it all. Helen's parents, William and Nellie Gallehue, had lost a son to pneumonia before Helen was born. After his death, her parents had four daughters of whom Helen was the second. Helen had good memories of growing up in Springfield, Illinois, where she was born.

When Helen was nine and a half years old her mother, Nellie, left the home to care for her sister who was suffering from tuberculosis (TB). TB was a very contagious disease

Ellsworth about the time of their wedding.

at the time and few survived. After her sister died, Nellie returned home, and soon after began showing symptoms of TB. By this time, sanatoriums were established to care for people with TB to help prevent the spread of the disease. Helen was only eleven when her mom went to Clifton Manor, a TB Sanatorium in Asheville, North Carolina, to recuperate from her disease. She regularly wrote letters to her four daughters and husband and bought clothes and other things they needed from a catalog. Helen's father went to stay nearby to be able to visit her. During that time, William's mother and his sister took care of the four girls: Dorothy, Helen, Wilma, and Suzanne. After three years at the sanatorium, Nellie died of tuberculosis. Helen was only fourteen when her mother passed away. Even though she had lived without a mother for so long, it was still devastating for her to lose her mother.

William soon remarried and Helen's new stepmother, Nettie, did not get along with the four girls, nor did they get along with her. Helen went to Minneapolis to live with her maternal aunt, Edna Basset, who became a great influence on her. Helen entered nursing school at St. Andrew's and it was here that she met Mike. Money was tight during the courtship. Because both of them were still paying for college, they decided to have a very small wedding. They were married in Simpson Methodist Church in Minneapolis. They had only two best friends as witnesses for them, Mary McMorran and Bill Bronner, and no other family or friends were present. Helen had no wedding dress, and no photos were taken. Helen said it was because of The Depression that they could not afford pictures or a wedding dress.

For their honeymoon, Mike and Helen drove to Washington State, where Mike's brother Bill and his family were living. It would save on expenses to stay with his brother while enjoying the beautiful sights of Washington. Helen's mother-in-law went with them so she could also visit Bill. Helen understood why her mother-in-law wanted to ride along but she was frustrated because Maude rode in the front seat next to Mike and Helen got the back seat!

Mike finished medical school on January 10, 1930, and began his internship at Ancker Hospital in St. Paul, Minnesota. Helen graduated from nursing school on June 4, 1930 and worked as a nurse to help support them. He was literally beginning his practice at the beginning of the Great Depression time period. Mike took great pride in his occupation and frequently took classes during his career to learn the latest procedures. Times were hard and many of his first patients paid him with commodities. Mike had to support not only his wife and mother, but also now his first child was on the way.

Ellsworth "Mike" Thayer college graduation, 1930.

University of Minnesota Medical School clerks at Glen Lake Sanitarium in 1929. Mike Thayer is pictured on the right.

Four Generations
Behind the Thayer Hotel in Annandale, Minnesota: David is held by his
father Mike. Grandmother, Maude Thayer is on the left, and on the right is his
Great-grandmother Caroline Thayer, who was managing the hotel.

5

Starting a Family
and Career

Mike and Helen were blessed with a baby boy born on September 17, 1931. They named him David Leroy after Mike's father. With Helen having full Irish ancestry and Mike over half Irish, it is little wonder that David inherited his parents' red curly hair.

The day after David was born, on September 18, Japan invaded Manchuria. The Pacific Theater of World War II had begun. The war against Japan would be a major influence on Mike's life as well as on the rest of the world.

An X-ray salesman whom Mike had met during his internship at Ancker Hospital in St. Paul knew of an opening for a doctor in Truman, Minnesota. The salesman suggested the two of them, along with Helen, go to Truman and look things over. Mike and Helen liked what they saw of Truman and decided to move there. The X-ray salesman sold the new doctor a used X-ray machine and all the equipment needed to get started. They became good friends, and through the years the salesman often stayed overnight with Mike and Helen when traveling in southern Minnesota. Mike moved his family to Truman and began his medical practice in July 1932.

Truman, a small rural community in southwest Minnesota, was established

Mike's office door in Truman, Minnesota. His son, David, is standing in the doorway.

in 1899. That same year, Dr. August Hunte became their first doctor serving the town from 1899 to 1930. Dr. Hunte left Truman in 1930 to start a medical practice on an Indian reservation. When Mike arrived in July 1932, he rented Hunte's building and moved his family into the front apartment of the building just behind his office. Otto Bang's family was living in the rear apartment. His son was also named Otto, and he was just two days older than David. The two became great friends, celebrated their birthdays together, and remained lifelong friends.

It was not easy to start a medical career during the Depression. Helen served as Mike's nurse at first. Office calls were $1.00, and house calls $3.00. Because local farmers had been hit hard by the Great Depression too, Mike was more than willing to agree to other forms of payment, such as baked goods, farm fresh eggs, and chickens. He kept good business records, recording every penny spent and earned and staying well within his budget. David recalled his father once buying him chewing gum and recording it in his ledger.

After living in an apartment in back of Mike's office for several years, the family built a home in the residential part of Truman. During that time, Mike had to do many home deliveries and house calls. In 1940, he decided residents of the area could benefit from having their own hospital. The closest hospital was in Fairmont about 14 miles south of Truman.

A large house was being remodeled on Ciro Street, a few blocks from where the family was living. Mike rented it for $10 a month and turned it into a hospital. He became licensed to run a ten-bed hospital. The operating room doubled as a delivery room. He hired three nurses, a head nurse and a cook. Dr. V.M. Vaughan, another doctor in Truman, also had patients in the hospital.

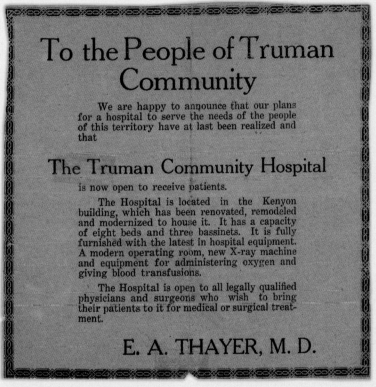

To the People of Truman Community

We are happy to announce that our plans for a hospital to serve the needs of the people of this territory have at last been realized and that

The Truman Community Hospital

is now open to receive patients.

The Hospital is located in the Kenyon building, which has been renovated, remodeled and modernized to house it. It has a capacity of eight beds and three bassinets. It is fully furnished with the latest in hospital equipment. A modern operating room, new X-ray machine and equipment for administering oxygen and giving blood transfusions.

The Hospital is open to all legally qualified physicians and surgeons who wish to bring their patients to it for medical or surgical treatment.

E. A. THAYER, M. D.

Newspaper announcement for the new Truman Hospital in the *Truman Tribune*.

David had many memories of growing up as a doctor's son. He recalled Mike doing all of his own lab work at home. The farm-fresh meat and produce that many patients offered in lieu of money more than proved to be a great benefit at home, since Helen was an excellent cook. The family ate like kings, David joked.

One day there came a knock at the front door, and when David opened it, a farmer carried half a hog into the kitchen. Laying it on the cutting board,

David and his pet chicken Pete.

he asked Helen how she wanted it butchered. He explained that Doc had accepted the hog as payment for his medical bill. When David was about six he walked through the office and saw a farmer fall to the floor from a heart attack. His father told him to quickly open the windows to get better air circulation. Because oxygen was not used then opening the windows was the next best thing.

Once a patient paid his bill with live chickens. David asked his dad if he could keep one chicken as his pet, and his dad agreed. David named his pet chicken Pete, and it followed him everywhere, even into the stores downtown. He loved his pet chicken. One day, David could not find Pete. He looked everywhere for him. That night his mom served chicken for dinner and as David looked at it he wondered where it came from. He could not eat it and felt sick, wondering whether this was his pet's fate. He never asked. He could not bear to think that his mother might have cooked his pet…but his Pete was never found. Sometime later his father confessed that they had served Pete for dinner.

David had several memories of growing up as a doctor's son. Once, when David was in elementary school, he went into the basement of his dad's office and saw the jars of body parts in formaldehyde, which his father used for study. David also recalls one time when his dad was having trouble with his car engine and was unsure how to fix it. It worked out great when the local mechanic needed medical care and could not pay with cash, so Doc agreed to "fix" him if he would "fix" his car.

Mike and Helen were active in many clubs such as bridge, the Masons, and church groups. Helen loved to cook and entertain. On many occasions, Helen prepared an elaborate meal just for the family, and when the elegant table was all set and ready for Mike, he would call from the office and tell them that work prevented him from making it home for dinner, because he had a house call to make, a baby to deliver, or some other emergency. Often the family ate without him. Helen attempted to keep food warm until he got home. David felt sorry for his mother, seeing how much work she put into cooking the meals.

Family Gathering
Helen was a great hostess and loved to entertain. The people in the photo are:
1. Son David L Thayer
2. Helen (Gallehue) Thayer
3. Martha (Thayer) Rochet (Mike's aunt)
4. Mary McMoran, a friend
5. George Rochet (Mike's uncle)
6. Aunt Minnie (Cooper) King, (Maude's sister). Minnie was the mother of Minnesota state auditor Stafford King.
7. Bertha King (Mrs. Stafford King)
8. Maude Thayer (Mike's mother)
9. Effie (Thayer) Walters (Mike's aunt), who managed the Thayer Hotel after Mike's grandparents retired
10. Grandma Caroline Thayer (Mike's step-grandmother, who originally managed the Thayer Hotel with her husband Albert Augustus).

David and William,
sons of Mike and Helen
Thayer.

Mike and Helen's second son, William Roger, was born in 1935 on Mike's birthday, June 12. William had several name sakes—Helen's father's name was William and Mike had a brother, uncle, and grandfather named William.

When this photo was published in the *Truman Tribune* on July 21, 1999, it was captioned "Truman's Second Hospital was managed by Dr. E.A. Thayer, now 91 and retired in Fairmont. Shown in the picture is Nurse Margaret Laube and husband, Mike in 1941." They decided if the photo itself was labeled "Margaret Laube and Mike", it could not be the doctor because his professional and legal name was E.A. or Ellsworth Albert. The photo was labeled with his nickname Mike so those who did not know the doctor assumed it was Margaret's husband Mike. The photo is correctly labeled on p. 159 of *Truman Centennial, 1899-1999; Proud Past, Promising Future*.

Dr. Mike Thayer with Nurse Margaret Laube in front of the Truman Hospital.

Mike started the Truman Community Hospital in 1940 which he owned and managed. He continued to use a sliding fee scale and reduced the medical bills based on patient's ability to pay. As shown by the two pictures, every year on Hospital Day, Dr. Thayer invited all the babies born at the hospital that year and their mothers to a picnic and to receive free immunizations that day. He gave his pastor free medical care because Mike felt that because the pastor was serving the Lord he should not have to pay for medical care. In 1943, when Mike was called into the service in World War II, he had to sell the first home he had built and move the family into the main floor of the hospital. They closed the hospital for business and used it as the Thayer's private home while he was away.

Hospital Day 1942

Hospital Day 1943

Family photo of Ellsworth, Helen, and sons William and David, taken in Truman, Minnesota.

6

LIFE AS A COUNTRY DOCTOR

On November 11, 1940, the worst snowstorm in Minnesota history—known as the Armistice Day Blizzard struck the area. Mike always made house calls when needed, and his patients knew they could depend on him. The following is excerpted from *Truman Centennial 1899-1999: Proud Past, Promising Future:*

> ...*During his practice, Dr. Thayer delivered over 3,000 babies. On one occasion, a farmer came to get him in a snow storm and they traveled with horses and a sled, over drifted fences and all to deliver a baby in the country. He spent the Armistice Day snowstorm staying overnight in Dr. Bailey's office in Fairmont. The next morning he knew he had to get back to Truman because one man had a broken arm and another lady was in labor. As he stepped outside, his hat blew off, so he went downtown in Fairmont to purchase a warm stocking cap. Dr. Thayer followed a snowplow out of Fairmont until about four miles from Truman, when the snowplow driver said he couldn't go on anymore. Dr. Thayer walked to the nearest farmhouse and asked to borrow a horse to ride to Truman. The farmer lent a farm work horse, and Dr. Thayer rode the horse bareback about another two miles to the home of Willard and Sadie Van Brunt. The horse kept breaking through the crusted snow and could not go on. Doc asked the Van Brunts to keep the horse until he could return it. They wanted to "keep" Doc too, but he insisted on heading to Truman and walked the last two miles so he could see his patients.*

Family photo of Ellsworth, Helen, and sons William and David, taken in Truman, Minnesota.

Mike fishing with his sons.   David and Bill having a riding lesson.

Mike loved going fishing with his sons, and hunting and golfing with them. He wanted them to learn to ride horses as he had. Because they did not own horses Mike arranged for a farmer to bring a horse into town and paid for his sons to ride the horse.

On June 18, 1941 Mike and Helen were blessed again with their third child and first daughter, Suzanne Alana Thayer. Helen's sister's name was Suzanne, and Mike's mother's middle name was Alana.

Noted on the Avenue—

The old saying "Youth will be served" was proved true by Doctor Thayer last Sunday. Mrs. Thayer and infant daughter Suzanne were ready and waiting for the doctor to take them to Mankato to catch the "400", crack flyer on the Northwestern line, while he was busy at the hospital bringing a baby into the world. Time was short for the 40-mile trip when Doc finally arrived, but he piled the luggage into the car while the good wife and Suzanne got seated and was off like Jehu. They reached Mankato in the nick of time. The train was ready to pull out on its fast run to Chicago. While Doc attended to tickets, porters hustled the baggage on board. The flyer pulled out. Doc, wiping the sweat from his brow, stepped into his car. Ye gods! There he saw a piece of luggage, the most important of all the numerous bags, cases and portmanteaus—Baby Suzanne's traveling bag. Without the things it contained the journey to Springfield, Ohio, would be a sore trial for both mother and daughter. Doc, who like all members of his profession is constantly called on for quick decisions, didn't hesitate. In a flash he was on his way to Waseca, 50 miles away, where the "400" makes a brief stop to take on passengers for Chicago and points east. Compared to Doc on that drive Barney Oldfield in his palmiest days was a mere Tyro.

Meanwhile on the train, Baby Suzanne had confidently followed the usual habit of infants by letting nature take its course. She wasn't worrying, but Mother was and likewise the porter when the necessary bag could not be located. He searched high and low but no dice. The train slid to a stop at the Waseca station. The porter stepping down from the vestibule saw a man on the platform holding a case. He recognized Doc, grabbed the piece, rushed into the pullman and with his face aglow cried triumphantly, Hyah it is, madam! Hyah is baby's duffle bag.

Mike and Helen's daughter Susie; with her red curly hair she looked like her Shirley Temple doll.

This is a cute news article written about Susie in the *Truman Tribune*. It shows the style of writing for the time period and shows a father's love and determination to take care of his family while being caught between his duties as a doctor and a father.

Bridge club at the Kanning home in Truman, Minnesota, in 1941. Dr. Herb and Merna Kanning were good friends with Mike and Helen and belonged to the same bridge club. Herb was a veterinarian. This bridge club night was hosted by the Kannings.

Mike's official military photo.

7

CALL TO DUTY

Historical events of the period

1940 – Rationing became the policy in America even before the country officially entered the war.

December 7, 1941 – Japan attacks Pearl Harbor.

December 8, 1941 – U.S. declares war on Japan.

December 11, 1941 – U.S. declares war on Germany and Italy.

August 7, 1942 – U.S. forces invade Guadalcanal.

In 1943 Mike was called into the Army. He sent notices to his patients asking them to pay their accounts before he left for duty. Patients were still charged only $1 for office visits and $3 for house calls. Mike closed the hospital during his service.

Cover of Mike's military-issued diary.

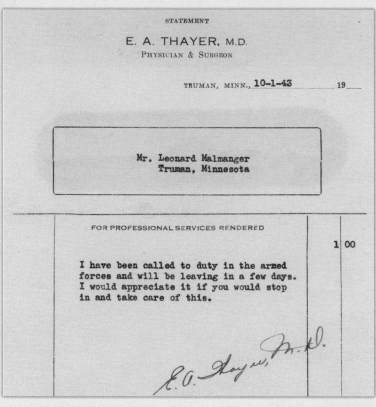

STATEMENT

E. A. THAYER, M.D.
PHYSICIAN & SURGEON

TRUMAN, MINN., **10-1-43**   19____

Mr. Leonard Malmanger
Truman, Minnesota

FOR PROFESSIONAL SERVICES RENDERED   1 | 00

I have been called to duty in the armed
forces and will be leaving in a few days.
I would appreciate it if you would stop
in and take care of this.

E. A. Thayer, M.D.

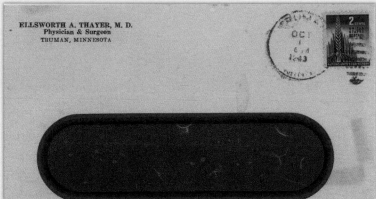

ELLSWORTH A. THAYER, M. D.
Physician & Surgeon
TRUMAN, MINNESOTA

A bill Mike sent before leaving for the Army. Postage in 1943 was 2 cents, and the bill was typed on the office stationery using a typewriter. About 2001, the bill eventually found its way into a box of assorted miscellaneous items sold at a garage sale in Truman. The man who bought it thought it would mean more to David Thayer and gave it to him.

Mike's service began on October 27, 1943, and he began writing in a military-issued diary.

Excerpts from his journal:

10/27/43 — Entered Train at 11:05 pm in Mankato Minn. Next day made numerous acquaintances including Hugo White representing Utah and Idaho Sugar Co., Mrs. Sorenson of Los Angeles, Harriet Evans. Mrs. Miller of Omaha who knows Dr. and Mrs. Hovel of Blue Earth. Met a Lt. Commander just reporting. Had been in Gen Practice in Nebraska. Changed trains at Omaha to Overland Limited. Stopover in Ogden of about 2 hrs. due to late train. Had breakfast between Ogden and Salt Lake. Arrived in Salt Lake City about 10:30 am on 10-29-43, Friday. To Fort Douglas[1] in officers car and delivered to officers mess. Thence to report and endless details. Got a room at B.O.Q.[2] then after bath etc. got into officers club for a beer and met Col. Harmon who assigns medical officers for 9th Service Command whom I had missed in the afternoon. He told me same as Col. Peters that my assignment to Oakland area Sta. Hosp. was a good break.

Ate dinner with a Lt. M.P.[3] from N.Y. then met a new Lt. Ordnance[4] with 16 months army and just transferring to Judge Advocate General Officer — he is a lawyer anxiously awaiting his first child Lt WH McElivee of North Carolina.

1. *Fort Douglas, near Salt Lake City.*
2. *BOQ is bachelor officer's quarters.*
3. *MP is military police.*
4. *Ordnance is a branch of the armed forces managing the supply and storage of weapons, ammunition, and related equipment.*

10/30/43 — Every one has been very kind and considerate to me a greenhorn. Met Lt. Carlson of Mpls, Minn a lawyer — ord. just transferred to Judge advocates office, a nephew of attorney Carlson of Blue Earth. Found out I was to report to Station Hosp. and offer my services (I got my first tetanus Toxoid there yesterday) so I reported to Major Ackerson who assigned me to Lt. Motchkan a swell egg— an internist——made ward rounds with him. Did a couple of histories and spent a couple of hours doing phys. exams in pm. Then watched him read x-rays till he was thru at 3:30. It has rained and snowed here all day. Got soaked feet once. Finally cleared up this afternoon.

10/31/43 Sunday — rounds in ward. 10:00 church, heard Col Blakely. Snow and slush. Saw Olsen and Johnson — Crazy House[5]

11/1/43 Monday — Worked at hospital and did physical exams. X-ray with Lt Matchan in PM. Cribbage 3rd night with Lt. Charles Carlson.

11/2/43 — Orders arrived and spent all day getting ready to go leave tomorrow for Oakland. Took in some of Salt Lake City today with Lt. who is going with me. Bought a foot locker. Show tonight with Lt. McElives "Lassie Come Home"

5. Crazy House was a 1943 movie starring Olsen and Chic Johnson with the Three Stooges that was made to give the military some comic relief. It is the only movie made with Frank Mitchell playing Moe Howard's part of Dumbo, joining Shemp Howard as Mumbo, and Fred Sandborn as Jumbo.

11/3/43 Wednesday — Awakened early as usual, showered etc. Met a Lt. Wilson dentist, Los Angeles just reported for duty. Went to hospital and checked out. Found a letter from Coles. Getting packed up, train due by 7:30 a. will leave at 3:30 P.M. so most of day to kill.

Finally took the train to SL left at 4:30 PM, on an old train. Got a lower berth and found it had been sold before but I was able to keep it. Accompanied by Lt. Stanley Tamowski, M.S.C. as far as Sacramento where he took train for Camp White Oregon. Had good night's rest. Wakened to beautiful trip thru Feather River Canyon on 4 Nov. Only two meals served on train and second one at 4 was Terrible. Beginning to get hot. 15 coaches 575 passengers — Sailors and Red Cross workers.

Arrived in Oakland 5:30 at Western Pacific Depot. No cabs, telephone, or transportation. Finally hooked a ride in a cab to Oakland Area Station Hospital (Old Oakland Hotel) and reported for duty at 6:30 pm to Maj. Throwell M.A.C.

who very graciously showed me around and settled in B.O.Q. (the old garage) — desolate — 5 bunks one room. Cement floor, sidewalk level, street cars in front.

Very very depressed —

No supper — so set out to walk around alone. Got a sandwich but couldn't eat — Sleep?

Family photo taken in Oakland, California in front of the house they rented near the Army hospital. David is dressed in his Boy Scout uniform.

8

OAKLAND, CALIFORNIA

11/05/43 — Report to duty. Assigned by Col. McEvers to 3 W. Septic Surgery under Col Newton. Currently under Capt. Randall, who spent the rest of day showing me around, Ended up with my head in a dither. But the situation is getting a little less repulsive.

I found more comfort in reading mother's testament tonight than in anything else. I thank the Lord for a Christian background in times like these to fall back on.

Tried to call Helen but would have to wait 3-4 hours and there is no phone in B.O.Q.

11/06/43 Saturday — Worked all AM on 3 W. Had chances to go to Pasadena with Maj Fainar, but few clothes. Tried to look up Stanley King[6], couldn't find him.

Met Col Ensign and wife, very nice. Looked at house to rent, Lt Cuhuy occupies, looks ok, $90 a month.

Back at post at 7. Guess I shouldn't have gone. Had hamburger and meats, milk for supper. And wrote to Helen. Then had a walk with Capt. Westerhoff — milk and donuts.

11/07/43 Sunday — got up at 6 am to call Helen. Got call thru in 5 mns. It was a thrill to hear the call go thru and hear their voices 6:40 am (8:40 CST) I choked up so I squeaked. They want to come out—Walked on air all AM— Worked thru to noon—and all P.M. till 4. Wrote Helen. Killed time and called land lady and rented house—all but details. I only hope the Good Lord delivers the folks safely out here. Finally went to a show alone.—I hate going to shows alone—"This is the army" glad I went—it killed an evening—broken in new shoes too.

11/08/43 Monday — Worked hard this A.M. Two hemorrhoids with Col Newton (Hitchcock and Yawarski) and a Thyroglossal duct cyst. Not much doing this afternoon — as went up town. Bought shirt and pink[7] got haircut. Tonight helped with two very acute appendices thru after 12 so another day killed but I think I learned a lot.

Had four air mail letters from Helen and one from mother. All in all a very good day.

6. *Lt. Stanley King was the son of Mike's cousin Col. Stafford King. Stafford King was a veteran of both world wars and served as the Minnesota state auditor, and the state commander of the American Legion, and headed the state department of soldier welfare. He served as a wing intelligence officer in the South Pacific and Fiji islands. Stafford's daughter, Elizabeth "Betty" King, served four years in the American Red Cross in England and Guam. She also sang with the United Service Organizations. Stanley King lost a leg in Pearl Harbor when his plane was clipped, in combat, crushing the leg and severing an artery. He plummeted to the ocean unconscious and near death from shock and loss of blood, and a crash boat rescued him. In the local newspaper, his mother thanked Red Cross blood donors for saving her son's life. After being released from the hospital, he returned to the Air Force as a link trainer instructor. Mike was able to visit with Stanley in the service and he was able to see Betty perform in the USO on one occasion.*

7. *Pinks were the name given for the army trousers (pants) issued during WWII. The olive drab semi-dress uniform was worn only by the Army officers and warrant officers. The uniform became informally known as the "pinks and greens" because of the contrasting scheme between the coat of Olive Drab shade 51 (dark green) and the pants of Olive Drab shade 54 ("pinks").*

11/12/43 Friday — Has been busy week and no mail since Monday. Minn. must have a blizzard. Have been fighting boredom and a typhoid shot evenings.

Worked daytimes — helped with thyroid, kidney, hemorrhoids. Am gradually learning duties as ward officer. Will soon take my turn as officer of day (Receive and admitting) Hope I hear from home. Saw a show again last night. Tested tonight and wrote letters.

11/15/43 Monday — Helen called yesterday — She plans on leaving home tomorrow. Nothing doing today everyone getting ready for inspection. Went up town today and arranged for phone and lights and gas. Yesterday walked up to house, it's a dirty mess but Mrs. McNutl said today man was going to paint and paper. Sat night I scrubbed as a peptic ulcer perforated, but turned out to be probably kidney stone.

Sat A.M. watched Col McEvers cauterize an epithelioma behind ear. Yesterday afternoon I went in and had a visit with him. Heard from Bill today. No mail from home and I miss it. This crowd of officers out here nothing like the gang at Douglas. You could laugh and have fun back there. Here everyone is trying to knife — or afraid of being knifed by someone.

The last journal entry above was on Saturday, which was probably November 20, 1943. The next entry was made over a year later on December 7, 1944. It is assumed that Mike's journal entries were made as much for his family to learn about his time in the service as for his own recollection. While the family was with him, there was no need to journal. These dates indicate that the family must have arrived in Oakland shortly after November 20, 1943. To help fill in the gap from this missing period, a copy of the hospital newspaper with Mike's name in it and one with an article about Helen's volunteer work with the Red Cross Auxiliary are included. An interview with David described what their life was like in Oakland during this time. The journal continues again on Dec. 7, 1944.

The U.S. Army commissioned this hotel in Oakland, California in 1942. It became known as the Oakland Area Station Hospital.

Dry Run, The Oakland Area Station Hospital Newsletter. According to the hospital newspaper, Mike enjoyed horsing around as a jockey!

Everyone did his or her part for the war effort. Helen is the second from the right pictured with the Oakland Chapter of the Red Cross Auxiliary in June, 1944. This auxiliary was made up entirely of the wives of the OASH officers.

This picture and caption is from the June 16, 1944 issue of *Dry Run*. Makers of surgical dressings: Seated L-R: Mesdames Viola McElligott, Stella Schwenk, Gertrude Smoody, Isabel Throwell, Jane MacMillan, Anna Jane Macklin, Ruth Lieberman, Marjorie Hayes, Pearl Schwartz, Germain St. Maurice, Trudy Hazen, Helen Thayer, Marvine Corso. Standing in back: Mrs. Beth Jennings, staff assistant; Mrs. Ann Hulett, vice chairman; and Mrs. Frances McEvers, chairman.

Memories of Oakland, California from Mike's son David

"It was a time of rationing and victory gardens. I remember saving gum wrappers and any cigarette wrappers, especially the Lucky Strike ones lined in tinfoil to keep it fresh. They recycled that tin liner to use in making bullets. When I was in California, I was in Boy Scouts; it was a big thing then. A lot of kids were relocated there so their families could work either in the shipyards, airplane factories, or were stationed there in the military. I met a friend in Boy Scouts, Bill Bradley from Arkansas, who had a feeding tube because he ate lye as a child. Dad was a friend of Bill's parents who worked in the airplane factory. The Scouts camped in the Redwood Forest when it was a new national landmark. I was in Boy Scouts before and after in Minnesota, too, for a total of six years. I was in Sea Scouts, too, in Truman. In Sea Scouts, we learned how to tie sea knots. I remember in California the ice man came twice a week. There was no fridge only an icebox. I was hired as my junior high school janitor for after-school hours. I also made extra money delivering the *Oakland Tribune*. I was eleven years old when I first moved to Oakland and thirteen years old when I moved back to Minnesota after the two years my dad was stationed there. My dad would help me deliver my route of papers on Sundays when he could. I always looked forward to spending that time with him. Henry J. Kaiser was a big shipbuilder before the war, and during the war he made the warships for the U.S. Navy. Postwar, Kaiser became a car builder. He was one of my customers. He later financed the Kaiser hospitals in California I believe."

Dave was asked if this paper route or his janitorial job was his first job, and he replied, "My first job was for Foster Drugstore back in Truman where I was a soda jerk, delivered prescriptions, and specialized in breaking fountain glasses," said with laughter. "Remember back then they didn't regulate child labor laws for the age you had to be to work."

Back to his recollection of living in California:

"I remember my dad took me to watch an operation at night at the Oakland

Hospital. I passed by rooms and saw many guys who were patients there; one had fingers hanging down caused by a fellow Marine using a machete and cutting him in a fight. Nurses gave me a footstool so I could see one operation…they laid his intestines on the stomach and found a secondary concern, and I remember them putting everything back in again. My parents loved to travel and every weekend we traveled to sightsee or visit family and friends. I remember how beautiful it was in the Yosemite area before all the population of today. There was a park in the middle of Oakland where I delivered papers to surrounding homes. They had boats for rent and the park was always busy with people there. There was a Navy man in a paddle boat who asked me if I wanted a ride. Nowadays you would have to be more cautious about strangers but back then it seemed fine. He was trying to enjoy his last day of leave and enjoyed talking to me. He said he was leaving the next morning for Europe and it was a dangerous mission and he would probably not make it home. He gave me $5 and said I reminded him of his son…and he knew he would never be home again to see him. I didn't know what to say but I have never forgotten that moment and often wondered what ever happened to him. A few weeks later I read in the paper about the D-Day invasion on June 6, 1944, and wondered if this was his mission in Europe for which he was leaving. It leaves an impact of how really brave these men were."

David collected military patches from people he met serving in the military while he was in California and sewed them on a sheet for display. Several are very rare.

David Thayer's collection of World War II patches.

Family photo taken in Oakland.

12/7/44 – Over a year has passed at Oakland Regional Hospital during this time I have been ward officer on Septic Surgery and most of time, Chief of Septic Surgery. Have assisted in General Surgery, orthopedics, G.U. and GYN

Served under Col Newton as chief of Surgery until June when Maj J.P. Schumaker took over. Capt. Kahlstrom, Riviera, and Randall were on surgery at start, in June shake up, Randall and I survived. Maj Claude Gates took over as chief of Gen Surgery and Septic Surgery. The experience has been very educational. Have assisted Capt Price on Gyn and Capt McElbgot on G.U.

Today I am alerted for overseas

12/17/44 – Started 15 day leave going to LA for 4 days to visit Strands and Smileys. Spent holidays with Helen, children, and grandma at home in Oakland – 490 Chetwood. Twas truly wonderful.

Returned to ORH 2 Jan 45 to 5W on Septic Surgery and more good surgical experience.

01/13/45 – Orders came to 309th General hospital – Fort Lewis. Left Oakland 25th Jan bt 16th St Sta [Station]– with Lt Wandke. Arrived in Tacoma 4 hrs later. Rode an ambulance to Ft Lewis via American Lake Vet Hosp. Spent 1st night in Bldg 400 an old barracks. Next a.m. was processed and sent out to 309th G.H. found them bivouacked[8] in woods. Bought fatigues and joined them.

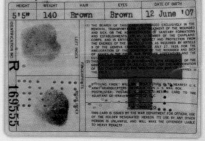

Mike's military ID.

01/28/45 — Helen's birthday — sent her a nite[9] letter last night.

Ate 2 meals from mess kit today. Tomorrow night sleep in tents.

8. A bivouac shelter is usually made of natural materials such as branches for support with leaves and plants laid on top to waterproof it for sleeping in a primitive camp area or in the mountains, used for scouting or the military. Bivouac sacks can also be used for sleeping out in the open.

9. A nite letter is a type of telegram with overnight delivery.

Bill and Clare came out this eve. Took me to Olympia — truly was nice. A letter to folks and to bed — got a letter from them yesterday.

Well the bivouac was a howling success — under Black Out Conditions. Fun now that is over but the cold, rain and coal soot was very unpleasant at the time.

02/03/45 Friday — Learned tonight that I might get TPA as troop train is crowded. That way could take folks home.

02/04/45 Saturday — got TPA now for plane reservation. Bill and Clare came after Joe and I went to Olympia then I spent week end with them. Gen Foster got plane reservation for me to Oakland on United Air Lines.

02/05/45 Sunday — Went out and visited Geo and Wilma — very nice P.M. Bill brought me back to Lewis in evening.

02/06/45 — Spent last night with Bill and Joe Wandke also. Took the 7:50 am plane for Oakland. Joe leaves at 11. My first real plane ride. It was swell. Stopped at Portland and Sacramento. Got to Oakland at noon and was delivered to O.R.H. My car was there and imagine Helens surprise when she and Dave bumped into me in the hall.

Got gas and transportation straightened out. I spent rest of day and night packing.

02/07/45 — 8:30 am departed for Truman. The 5 Thayers in a Ford. All went well till we left Sacramento and started to climb — finally decided it was due to a plugged radiator precipitated by anti-freeze, but by stopping at every *station and driving slow on climbs were able to keep going. Thru Donners Pass about 4 PM. Drove all night except for catnaps. The kids slept well, cold at times. Arrived at Salt Lake City at noon after breakfast at Winnemucca. Got a new radiator and flat tire fixed and dinner. Left at 3:30 drove till late 8 or 9 and stopped at Rock Springs, Wyoming. Had supper and 2 rooms at hotel. Left at 8:30 am.*

I drove all day to stop about 8 PM at North Platte Nebraska. Got started about 8 AM.

02/10/45/ Saturday — Home in Truman at 5 PM.

Had a glorious week in Truman — own home church — kids in school and with their toys and friends — old friends — for the kids it was just like Christmas and for us a happy homecoming.

02/16/45 Friday — Kannings took us and David to Mpls — sis stayed in Truman to look after things. Went shopping with Dave. Cocktails at Schieles, dinner at Radisson and night at Patters.

02/17/45 — 7AM took plane for Chicago arriving at 8:55 and waited till 12:30 for plane to Atlanta arriving at 7 PM. Then waiting till 10:30 to take off for Columbia arriving about 12 am and got to bed in B.O.Q about 2 am.

02/18/45 — Joe and I took in Atlanta, quaint — fun.

Dr. Thayer and Dr. Joe Wandke had first met in Oakland and later in South Carolina they discussed plans for work after the war. They later became partners in a medical practice in Fairmont, Minnesota. Their wives also became friends. Mike took some 8mm film footage of the two families enjoying a park and of the college in South Carolina where they trained.

Mike and Helen while in Truman, Minnesota when Mike was on leave.

First Lieutenant Ellsworth Albert Thayer and wife, Helen.

9

FORT JACKSON, SOUTH CAROLINA

On December 7th Mike was alerted that he would be going overseas to Tinian Island. He was sent to Fort Jackson, South Carolina for training. There was no telling how long Mike might be stationed away from his family in Tinian Island, so Helen wanted to go to SC with him while he trained. Their two sons, David and Bill, stayed with Herb and Merna Kanning in Truman so they could attend school. Dr. Kanning, was a local Veterinarian and family friend. After school, David often stopped at the home of another family friend, Mrs. Esther Cole for help with his homework. David recalls that she was very strict and always insured that his homework was done. Even in Minnesota, there were constant reminders of the war. David recalled: "I remember seeing German prisoners brought to the fairgrounds in nearby Fairmont (Minnesota) and kept in bunks often in the horse barns. Italian

Dr. Ray Sanford and Mike at Fort Jackson, South Carolina.

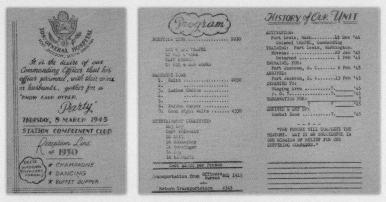

"Know Each Other" party invitation at Fort Jackson, South Carolina.

Group photo from basic training in South Carolina.

A close-up from the group photo. Mike is second from the right in the front row.

prisoners were very trusted and polite; they didn't want to fight for Hitler." Susie, who was not yet in school went to South Carolina with her mother.

02/25/45 Sunday — Went to church with Joe. Slept till 9 a.m. Talked to Helen Fri night and she called back last night. Believe she is coming out. Anyway I rented a room downtown for her. Have had one week of "Parallel" training at Fort Jackson Reg Hospital + Value + nill.

03/14/45 — Helen spent two weeks out here with me. Had a room in Columbia, S.C. It was glorious to have her here and fun roaming around this old Southern town — Sure miss her since she left on the 12th. (arr about 23 Feb).

Our parallel training is over so are marking time for a while. Work in hospital part of time. Very little drill, exercises value so far — still nil. (Broke L. great toe oh my)

Wandke is my roommate — swell fellow and helps break the monotony. The whole outfit are nice. Price is here from Oakland also. Hope we get going soon although this is a nice place and climate. The inactivity is trying.

It finally developed that our orders for F.T.O. were cancelled about 4 days prior to our departure. We were to have gone to Camp Joyce Kilmer N.J. Easter Sunday, (last of March). So we sat.

Helen visited me in Feb and Mar for 2 weeks and as we sat doing nothing Dan Webster and I looked around. I found a house nice little bungalow with 3 bedrooms, radio, Frigidaire and gas stove for $100/mo. So we took it. 21st of April and a few days later Lee and David (Stinky) Webster moved in. Helen and Suzanne arrived a couple of days later Fri (Apr 27). At the time I was on OB GYN Service with Maj. Harrel and on call every other night. So we spent alternate evenings at the Fort but were able to sleep at 3210 Monroe St. I soon got off OB and spent a lot of time loafing and pleasant evenings at home, bridge etc. Suzanne was swell, it was wonderful to have her there. She became a pal of Kay Taylor whose folks lived 2 doors away. We met some nice people, neighbors and rather enjoyed life in the South — in retrospect.

Webster's folks came down for a visit and on Easter Sunday.

05/13/45 — I received notice of my Promotion — as of May 11, Capt. Thayer. Only 19 ½ mo of active duty as a Lt. Gives one an idea of my true worth to the Army.

We knew our readiness date was somewhere in mid-June. And June 1 I asked for a leave and imagine my surprise to get 8 days. Mother had written that David was getting more stooped and tired all the time. She took care of things while Helen was in S.C.

So Fri noon (June 1) Helen and Sue got on the train for home. And I with a priority got on the plane at 1 am Sat. June 2. Again I got airsick, and by Chicago it was cold. I had left hot SC in cotton khaki. Got off at Rochester at 1:30 PM when I found I could get a bus home in an hour. Changed to wool clothes and blouse and arrived in Mankato about 4:30. Where Grandma, Gertrude and a couple of the dandiest boys in the world met me. They had a new pup, Toots.

Sunday noon we met Helen and Sue in Mankato, after fixing a flooded basement Sunday a.m. Then began the happiest week of my life. Just to hang around with my loved ones in our own home. Chickens, garden, pup, pigeons, and a lawn, cleaning the basement, all the things that a man enjoys with his kids. To say nothing of wonderful friends dropping in.

And suddenly it was Sat. night and time to go to Mpls. We left after midnight. Gertrude went along to drive back. My plane left about 5 a.m. I believe. In Chicago I changed to cotton again. I arrived in Columbia near midnight. Air travel still makes me sick.

06/10/45 — Billy and I celebrated our birthdays jointly and prematurely on Fri the 8th and we played a lot of croquet on Bill's new set. Had X-rays taken of David which I took back with me.

06/11/45 — X-ray & Orthopedists say Dave has a dorsal epiphysitis so will arrange to have him go to Rochester.

First Lieutenant Ellsworth Albert Thayer and wife, Helen.

First Lieutenant Ellsworth Albert Thayer and wife, Helen.

David holding Toots with his sister Susie and brother Bill.

06/12/45 — Lee had Joe and I out for my birthday with a nice cake and a swell evening. They are darned nice people.

06/18/45 Monday — We depart from Ft Jackson on a troop train. I am car commander for an officers' Pullman. All in all the trip was not bad. Weather was good. Meals fair and dirt plentiful. The scenery was great, we went to Atlanta thru Tennessee to St. Louis, then up to Mpls via Southern Minn (Albert Lea) but hit that at night. Awakened in AM in Mpls. Then bus straight across Minn on G.N. via Willmar — boy, the state looked wonderful, if wet. Glacier Park and the mountains were beautiful. Arrived Sat. 23 June in Seattle and by truck to Ft Lawton, where we were processed all thru the week and called Bill Sun and he, Clare and Babs came out and had supper with me at the Club.

Mon night to my surprise, we got passes and Joe and I went to Seattle. Called Gen Foster who picked us up and took us to see Claudia and Rosemary for a few minutes then out to his place. Then he and Wilma took us out to Bills and then back to Ft Lawton.

06/27/45 Wednesday — we boarded the USS Tazewell APA 209 309th first, followed in afternoon by 304 and 310. I started out as Compartment Commander for Comp 4 — 302 E.M. packed in 4 deep. Thu PM I picked Klejsnowiez as an assistant and promptly began to get seasick and didn't care whether I died or not. We had abandon ship drill. Slept in a tight ward room, blackout and all. 1st two nights were not bad but from thence it was hot. Stopped 24 hours at Enewetak Atoll for refueling after crossing the International Date Line and losing June 6th.

MY LIFE
IN THE
SERVICE

THE DIARY OF

Ellsworth Albert Thayer

0535509

1st Lt. M.C.A.U.S.

11 May 45. Capt MC

Mike labeled this photo of himself with Rev. Bill Ackerman as "The Doc and The Chaplain."

10

TINIAN ISLAND

Docked at Tinian on Sat. 14 July 45 I went by truck to central part of island to the old 112th CB area where we moved into tents. My tent mate and I — Capt. Bill Ackerman, Chaplain — Presbyterian promptly began scavenging for furnishings. Found chairs and benches. There was a table also cans of food. Details were putrid and boy scoutish. 3rd and 4th day Joe burned his hand and was hospitalized for 2 — 3 weeks.

The renowned Seabees were the Navy Construction Battalion. The name Seabees came from the initials CB. Their official motto is: Construimus, Batuimus - which means "We Build, We Fight." During World War II, 325,000 men served with the Seabees on six continents and more than 300 islands building major airstrips, roads, bridges, Quonset huts, hospitals, and housing. They often landed with the Marines to dismantle enemy road blocks. On June 6th, 1944, D-Day, the Germans had placed barriers on the beaches of France, and the Seabees dismantled enough of them to allow the Higgins boats to land. On Tinian Island the Seabees built the major airstrips needed to fight Japan. The *Enola Gay* took off from those airstrips on its way to bomb Hiroshima. In the Pacific Theater they built 111 major airstrips needed to reach Japan, 441 piers, tanks for storing 100m gallons of fuel, barracks to house 1.5 million military and hospitals for an estimated 70,000 patients.

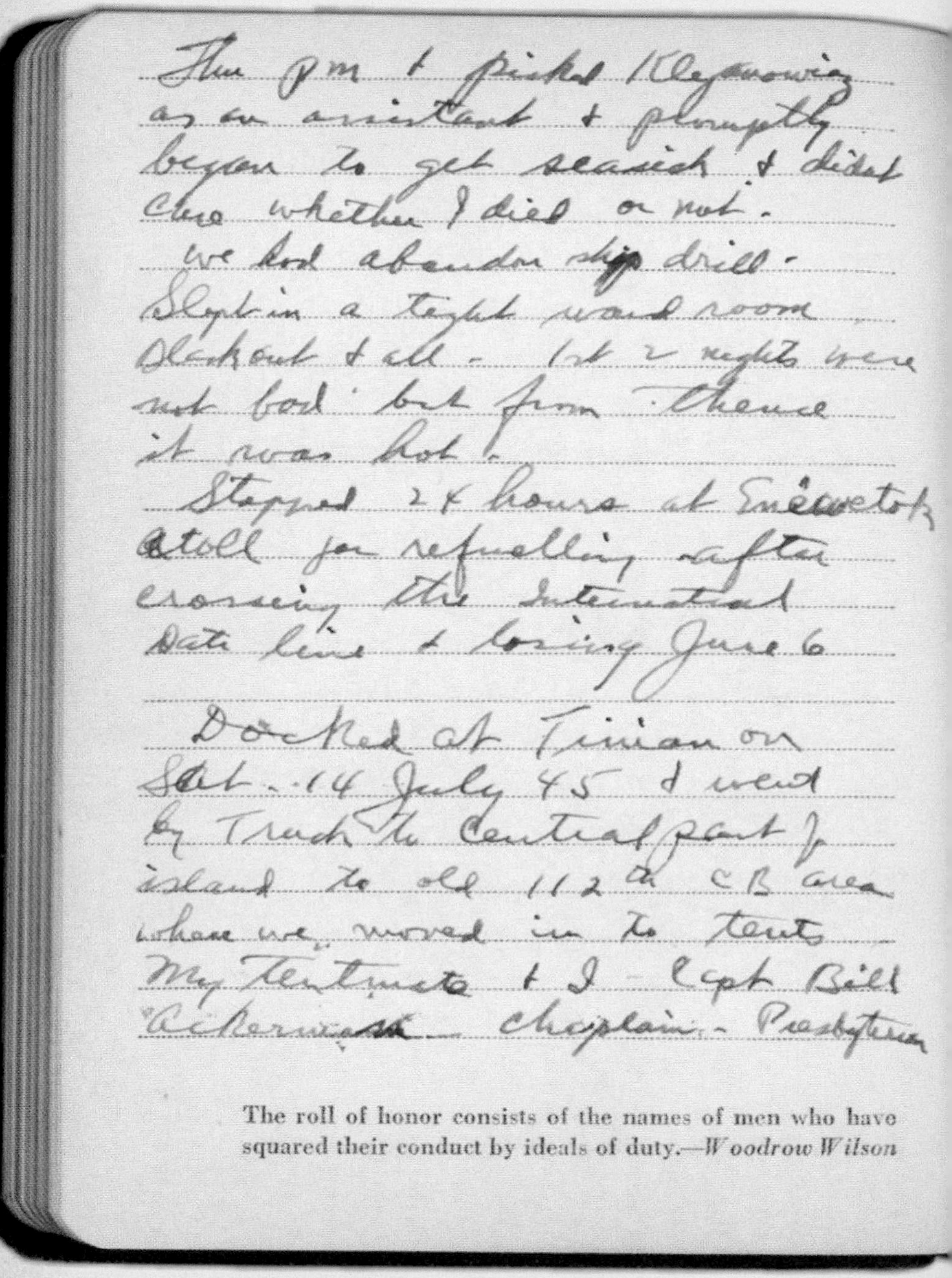

This pm I picked Klejnowicz
as an assistant & promptly
began to get seasick & didn't
care whether I died or not.

We had abandon ship drill.
Slept in a tight ward room
blackout & all. 1st 2 nights were
not bad but from thence
it was hot.

Stopped 24 hours at Eniwetok
atoll for refuelling after
crossing the International
Date line & losing June 6

Docked at Tinian on
Sat. 14 July 45 & went
by truck to central part of
island to old 112th CB area
where we moved in to tents
My tentmate & I - Capt Bill
Ackerman - chaplain - Presbyterian

The roll of honor consists of the names of men who have
squared their conduct by ideals of duty.—*Woodrow Wilson*

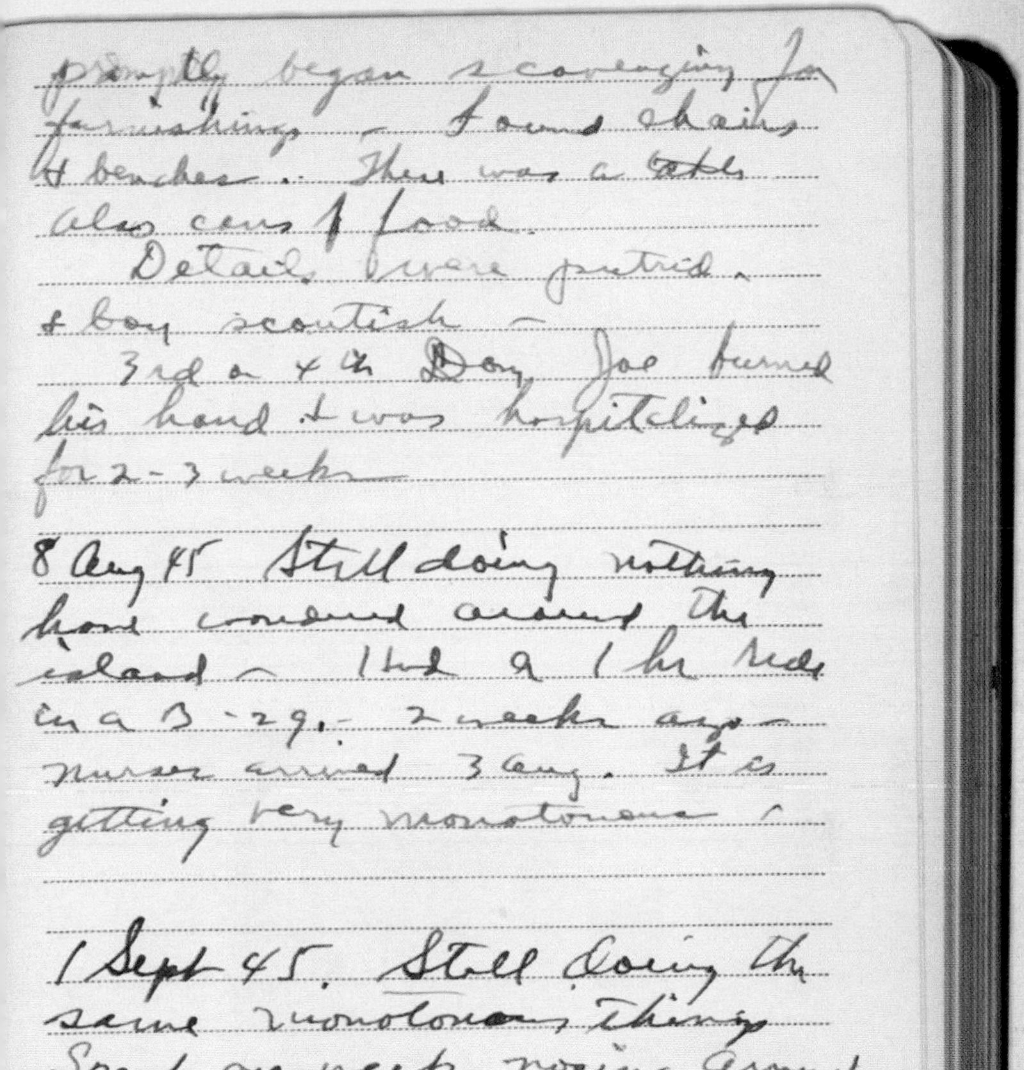

promptly began scavenging for
furnishing — found chairs
& benches. There was a table
also cans of food.

Details were putrid —
& boy scoutish —

3rd & 4th Day Joe burned
his hand & was hospitalized
for 2-3 weeks

8 Aug 45 Still doing nothing
have wandered around the
island — Had a 1 hr ride
in a B-29. — 2 weeks ago
nurses arrived 3 Aug. It is
getting very monotonous —

1 Sept 45. Still doing the
same monotonous thing
Spent one week nosing around

Our country! in her intercourse with foreign nations may she always
be in the right; but our country, right or wrong!—*Decatur*

Many of the captions for these photos came from Mike's own handwriting on the photos.

The Doc and Chaplain's Tent.

Mike labeled this photo of Bill Ackerman, himself, Joe Wandke, and an unknown man as "Bunker, Ackerman, Thayer, and Wandke."

CB's laying out the coral pathways.

Left to right: Rev. Bill Ackerman, Webster, Dr. Ray Sanford, and Dr. Mike Thayer. The pathway was made of coral topped with asphalt. CB's (Seabees) used the same for runways.

B-29 coming in for a landing over our tent.

Shinto Shrine reconstructed by CB's. Most of the original was badly damaged.

This American temporary cemetery was near Invasion Beach on Tinian and contained more than 600 combat and operational casualties.

Shinto Shrine at Broadway and 110th Street on Tinian under construction by Japanese prisoners and the CB 110 Battalion.

The sign reads "Japanese War Dead Cemetery #2," Tinian Island.

Line outside enlisted men's mess hall.

Interior of the enlisted men's mess hall in the 309th Hospital area.

The 310th General Hospital area as seen from the observation tower. Saipan is in the distance.

The 309th officers' mess, officers' club and billet as seen from the observation tower.

Enlisted men's mess hall and area as seen from the observation tower, with the cliffs in the background.

Headquarters of the 309th General Hospital.

Officers' laundry in operation.

The Showers! Major Wilson.

The U.S. Army Air Force's Eighth Air Force tail insignia shows this plane with the "W" tail marking in a circle signifying that it is part of the 489th Bomb Squad of the 2nd Bomb Division.

Left to right: Bill Ackerman and Mike with some medium size (500 lb.) bombs.

The 309th General Hospital Photo Shop which supplied a complete photo service to all members.

08/08/45—Still doing nothing have wandered around the island—Had a 1 hr. ride in a B-29 2 weeks ago. Nurses arrived 3 Aug. It is getting monotonous.

A typical residence of the Mariana natives on Tinian.

On New Year's Day American service men handed out chocolate bars to the Tinian children.

Tinian Island children.

09/01/45 – Still doing the same monotonous things. Spent one week nosing around a ship, unloading detail. One night on guard and one week on the construction battalion building the hospital on the hill Quonset[10] huts

10. *A Quonset hut is a prefabricated portable hut with a semicircular roof of corrugated metal that curves down to form walls. This is used by the military because it can be quickly assembled.*

Skeleton of a Quonset hut in the 309th area. Left to right: Ray Sanford, Joe Wandke, and Bill Ackerman.

Joe was hospitalized nearly 3 weeks.

We have added screens to our tents. Now have a laundry detail to do our laundry. The officers club has been fixed up quite nice. Beer is rationed to 6 cans a week and 5 cokes. Bill gets the cokes and I the beer. Also joined the Tasa locker club (Deposit $40) and can buy 1/5 a week tax free and fairly good—Seagrams V.O. 1.30

Film actor Charlie Ruggles and fellow cast members with officers of the 309th. Ruggles was in over 100 films during his career – five in 1941 alone. During World War II he devoted much of his time to the war efforts and appeared in only 3 films during the next three years. He entertained troops in the Pacific and spent up to 5 consecutive months overseas with them. At home he sold war bonds and auctioned off the clothes he wore in movies to help fund the war effort. In this group photo, Mike, who is standing behind the second man on the right (kneeling), appears to be looking at Ruggles.

Building a sand patio outside the officers' club.

309th area with club and officers' mess hall.

Interior view of the officers' club of the 309th General Hospital.

Interior view of the officers' mess hall with kitchen personnel.

Have acquired some shell necklaces and aluminum beads for the kids. Souvenirs are scarce. Nurses arrived about 2-3 weeks after we did and live in 303rd area so we see very little of them except a few of the "faithful". The air Corps looks after the rest. Have been going to 38th CB for movies each night and now one is starting in our own area.

View of No. 88, a B-29 named *Up an' Atom* part of the 509th CG.

Mike standing by the sign to the Entrance to 38th Seabees' area.

Colonel Paul Tibbets flew the *Enola Gay* carrying the bomb, code-named "Little Boy." The original tail marking of the 509th B-29s was the forward-pointing arrow in a circle. The 509th was the unit that carried out the atomic bomb mission. In order to avoid being recognized by Japan as a plane able to carry the atomic bomb, just prior to August 6th the tail marking was changed to the circle-R, which was the marking for the 6th Bomb Group, 313th Wing, North Field, Tinian. After the mission the arrow in a circle was repainted on the tail. After Japan surrendered the top of the vertical stabilizer was tipped in red along with the circle arrow. When the *Enola Gay* was put on display at the Smithsonian they repainted the markings to represent the way it was at the time of the atomic mission. The Enola Gay is on display with the circle-R marking in the National Air and Space Museum's Steven F. Udvar-Hazy Center in northern Virginia. Mike's photo is a rare one taken before the mission. The B-29 named *Bockscar* #77 of the 393d Bombardment Squadron, 509th Composite Group carried the second atomic bomb code-named "Fat Man," that destroyed 44% of the city Nagasaki.

The *Enola Gay*, B-29 number 82 which dropped the first atomic bomb on Hiroshima.

> There was a week's suspense following the atomic bomb reports and anxious waiting for the Japs to surrender. We finally got the word at 9am on 14 Sept during a medical meeting. It broke up — there was no hilarity and probably more tears of joy than shouts. Our men came off the hill at noon on order of CO, but were sent back by his superior to continue useless construction and continue it they did for another 2 weeks.

The cities of Hiroshima and Nagasaki were hit by atomic bombs in 1945. This map shows their location.

The timings of his journal entries are interesting. Mike arrived on Tinian on July 14 and writes about the monotony. Hiroshima was bombed on August 6th and Nagasaki on August 9th. On August 8th Mike still writes that he is doing nothing and it is getting monotonous. Japan surrendered on August 15th and the war officially ended on September 2nd when the Instrument of Surrender was signed. On September 1st he is still complaining about the monotony, it was not until September 14th that the news of the surrender was given to him in a meeting. Although the planes took off from Tinian Island for the atomic bombings, only a select few on the island knew about the secret Manhattan project.

We have had medical and surgical meetings and discussions about 5 mornings a week and EKG classes three times a week. Other than that writing and reading have been about the only monotony breakers. Some of the fellows go swimming a lot but that is mostly sun bathing due to coral. Others have puttered with wood work, shells, etc. I made a folding chair and bed side table for myself. Work out here is very exhausting due to the oppressive humidity — rain comes 2 — 3 times daily.

The Captain in his chair

In Mike's journal he mentions making a chair; this is probably the chair he made. The next photo shows a bedside stand that he made. He was bored and believed it was a waste of time to be on an island that had little need for a doctor. No one yet knew about the Manhattan Project and how soon his medical services would be needed.

Mike at work in Tinian.

Tinian Beach (South Beach), restricted to enlisted personnel.

09/01/45 — I've been having a lot of gastric distress. I tried to get a GI series. I'm getting it but have to enter the hospital tomorrow. I'll bet it takes me a couple of weeks before I am out.

Hospitalized 3 days. Results negative.

09/17/45 — went on "choosy" diet and no alcohol or tobacco & atropa belladonna & amphojel

10/10/45 — I met Jim Fitch a few days after his arrival and attachment to 313th wing. We had a few pleasant excursions together, exploring Jap caves, collecting souvenirs etc.

A soldier standing by the entrance to one of the caves where the Japanese hid. Large coral caves contained a blasted Japanese howitzer, the bodies of Japanese who had committed suicide, and unexploded shells. This cave is connected to other caves by a honeycomb of passages, shell stairways and companionways.

Coastline scene near Suicide Cliff.

The Pacific Ocean and the lower cliffs with Marpo Point in the distance. This point which was dubbed "Suicide Cliff" is just above some of these caves.

Mike is standing in the front, near the edge of Suicide Cliff, wearing a white T-shirt.

Several thousand Japanese and Korean soldiers and civilians jumped to their deaths off Suicide Cliff as American Marines surrounded them. Nearby patrol boats broadcast requests to surrender, but the Japanese people believed they would be tortured. They threw their children over the cliff and then jumped after them.

Plateau and Suicide Cliff from the upper cliff. The small dots are trucks.

Ray Sanford and Bill Ackerman beside prehistoric ruins in Old Tinian Town.

Shinto Shrine – Sanford, Thayer, Richmond.

Friends at entrance to Japanese monument.

Two 309th nurses on a sight-seeing tour of a Japanese monument.

Camp Churo, an internee camp.

Camp Churo

Author's Comments

If a picture says a thousand words, then this picture is misleading of what Camp Churo was actually like. Fifty years after World War II, we have learned in our history classes that the internee camps were a cruel way to treat the Japanese people. While some poor living conditions and mistreatment may have happened in other internee camps that I do not know about, I want to play the devil's advocate and give a true perspective of life in Camp Churo. Keep in mind that in all wars after a country takes over another country, the local people may still have loyalties to the enemy side so they need to be contained temporarily until the end of the war. Think about the Americans who are now living on the island temporarily until the end of the war. There are many locals who were not captured and are hiding in the caves along the shore line acting as snipers shooting the American soldiers as they walk among the beach or cliff areas.

The Americans established Camp Churo for Tinian's nonmilitary residents that originally numbered 10,635. The camp was ironically misnamed "Camp

Churo" by the U.S. military who built it inside the Tinian village of Chulu. The U.S. chose the site because of the existence of water wells. The American Foreign Economic Administration's farm program worked hard to clear the fields on Tinian from the hazardous debris and make the soil rich for planting again. Needed farm equipment was brought in. Up to 170 civilian Japanese and Korean men and women tilled the soil with the help of 100 U.S. Navy men, under the direction of the FEA. Seed was sent over from America, and the field size was increased to 3,000 tillable acres. The people living in Camp Churo who were farmers worked the land; the fishermen were allowed to leave the camp and go out and fish. The population quickly rose to 11,479 with 9,000 Japanese and Okinawan civilians, four Chinese, and the remainder Koreans. There were no Chamorros or Carolinians in the civilian count. The birth rate was four times higher than the death rate. Residents were guaranteed two meals a day and those who volunteered to work were given a third meal at noon. They were encouraged to engage in a variety of small labor projects for the military.

Handicrafts at the camp included weaving, and making dolls, wooden masks, miniature wooden models of the native cow carts (karetan guaka) that date back to the Spanish period, woven pandanus bags, jewelry, belts, and other articles that were sold through post exchanges and ships' stores. The workers received island wages.

An educational program began in October 1944 and was attended by 92% of the Japanese children and 98% of the Korean children with a total enrollment of 2,500. Eighty-one native teachers joined the U.S. military teachers and conducted the classes in about fifteen large tropical buildings. Students studied their native languages, English, arithmetic, natural science, and calisthenics. An excellent Boy and Girl Scouts program was developed at Camp Churo. Paid leadership was provided for the program. It was administered by the American personnel, but the details were run by the local civilians. There were 16 troops with a total of 800 scouts. A playground was built in the middle of the camp as well. A Quonset hospital housing 110 beds was built in the camp. It employed seven doctors and 55 native nurses. Three of the doctors were Japanese and had previously practiced in Tinian Town. The American military provided needed medical supplies and assistance.

Freedom of worship was exercised at Camp Churo. Two Buddhist priests lived there with a large Japanese following; there was a Catholic church of 56 members and two Protestant churches of approximately 600 members. A Community Chest program raised approximately $1,000 a month to fund relief and constructive programs in the community. After the war ended, America returned the island to the Mariana people and rented the airstrip from them. The local Mariana people were so grateful to America who helped free them from being ruled by Japan. This is evident by the Mariana Medal they give out now to the servicemen who helped free them as seen at the end of this book.

When this camp is compared to the concentration camps of Germany or to the POW camps in Vietnam, Americans can be proud that the natives were treated with dignity even under dire circumstances and given so much assistance in recovering from the war.

Saipan as seen from a hill on Tinian Island.

Rubble and wreckage on White Beach No. 1, showing antiaircraft gun and torpedoes.

10/10/45 — a ship arrives with orders to take us to Sasebo & 308 to Kure. We have no orders so there are a few days of confusion culminating on our departure 22 Oct Mon.

Sunday a movie film arrived & I had Jim's camera so amid the confusion of packing I tried to expose a film then a rain came up & the last few feet were given to Jim to expose. He helped me pack my bed roll.

During the stay on Tinian I sent home 3 boxes of "crap" and still have too much stuff to carry. The departure of many air corps & Seabee units gave us more comforts in the way of beds etc. I got a hospital bed & mattress to enjoy the last week. Sneaked a visit to Camp Churo one day and got a few pictures.

It is assumed that the following photos, all numbered in the lower right-hand corner, were taken by military photographers on Tinian Island. Mike kept them in his box of photos. The descriptions of each are taken from a list which accompanied the photos.

Japanese fortress on North Air Strip showing the marks of battle. After the invasion, we used it as an engine repair shop for B-29s.

A B-29 starting on a bombing mission headed for Tokyo.

A view of the harbor constructed by the U.S. Navy. This harbor is enclosed by submarine net, and has enough docks that ten large ships may be uploaded at one time.

Wrecked American amphibious tanks near the Invasion Beach.

An overall view of North Field showing many B-29s, with Saipan rising out of the Pacific Ocean in the distance.

B-29 graveyard showing many planes wrecked on this island in operational accidents.

309th nurses doing laundry in their own area.

Wrecked Japanese tanks on the south side of the island near the harbor.
These tanks were disabled by low-flying aircraft during the invasion.

Wreckage of the only village on Tinian Island — Tinian Town.

View of Japanese civilian driving an ox-cart. This is the ordinary type of transportation used by inhabitants of this island. Picture taken in the men's section of Camp Churo

Entrance to 50th Seabee area showing beautiful flowers and a mounted Japanese naval gun.

Newly constructed officers' club of the 444th Bomb Group. The enlisted men have a club which is very similar, about a half-block away.

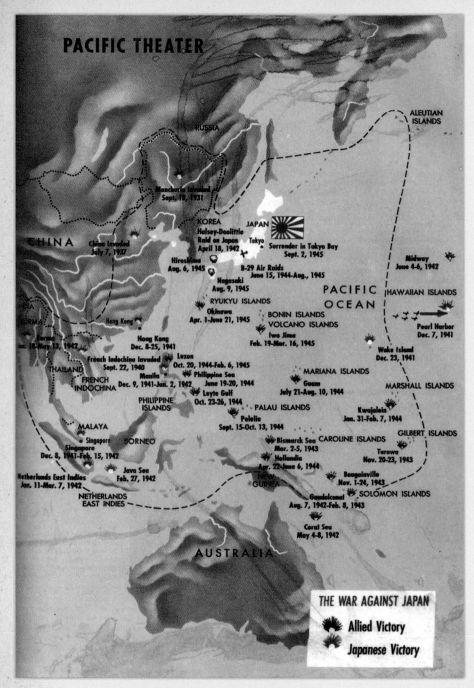

This map summarizes the war against Japan.

The allied victories as shown on the map provided a corridor through the middle of the Pacific Theater, which was crucial in winning the war. This middle path enabled the allies to build air strips on the islands in order to refuel and make the trip to Japan. Many of these islands in the corridor were won by the allies in hard fought battles.

Leaving Tinian for Fukuoka after bombing Japan, the U.S. government sends its medical unit from Tinian to Fukuoka to assist the Japanese in providing medical care.

"Let us pray that peace be now restored to the world and that God will preserve it always."
— General MacArthur, after Japan signed the Instrument of Surrender aboard the USS Missouri

Being saluted by Japanese after their surrender.

11

Fukuoka, Japan

10/22/45 — 1PM after a trip to the docks in trucks, then via LCVPs (Higgins boats) we boarded the USS Gage APA168. The 308 GH having filled the ship with their cargo we were limited to T.A.T & personal luggage. Nurses had the dormitory & #1 compartment. We had #2 just below them in the bow of ship & ate in #3 just below that.

Tues AM I got seasick. The trip was rough & there was more pitching than I could tolerate. Thu I was better but Thu PM a storm came up & I was really sick.

Fri AM we were in the Straits to China Sea & I really enjoyed breakfast. That afternoon we anchored in the China Sea 7 miles from Kure and next day started unloading cargo in LCVPs to the island on which the Jap Naval Academy stood & which the 308th was to occupy.

On October 24, 1945, the United Nations was established. It first met in January 1946 in London.

10/27/45 — Two years in Army.

10/28/45 Sunday — 8:30 I squeezed into a line going aboard one of the LCVPs & had a beautiful ride. Then a quiet sea with Jap fisherman here and there. Small Jap villages along the shore. Saw bombed out Kure in the distance with a skeleton ship yard smoking still. We passed 4 sunken Jap War ships & 2 carriers afloat

Aboard the L.C.V.P.
Tinian in background.
McDonald, Yuenler,
Coley, Stearns.

USS Gage APA168 as we left her in Sasebo Harbor.

The Skeleton Ship Yard is Still Smoking!

The beauty of the sea with the steep mountainous islands arising from it is hard to describe. The weather was perfect too. We got off at a small wharf walked thru a mob of kids to enter at the gates of Naval supply warehouses — where I got my 1st Jap salute. Boarded a nice Jap rt hand drive bus driven by G.I. & rode for 2 – 3 mi to the Naval Academy which had beautiful big buildings & campus. I strolled thru the area till 11. Ate C Rations for dinner and caught a truck back to the landing area. Wandered thru the naval warehouses then caught an empty LCVP which got me back to the ship at 1 P.M. in time for ice cream. I brought aboard a Jap bugle from the academy which I hope to get home.

Skeleton ShipYard.

Written on seven sheets of thin onionskin paper using a feather quill pen is the following letter that Mike wrote home to Helen. He wrote on both sides of the paper and drew an explanatory map to give her an idea of the surrounding area he is describing in his letter to her.

This letter was shared with Mike's mother Maude who had it published in the
Clarrisa, Minnesota newspaper.

10/28/45 Sunday 5:30 PM

Dear Helen,

*Every time I open my writing kit I see your picture, I'm so grateful for it. Then
I look at the snaps of the kids and I get homesick — but that isn't what I started
to write.*

*Yesterday Dan and 3 others went ashore with some of the cargo. Everyone else
was stopped. So last night we were all trying to figure angles we could work to
get ashore. Well the CO decided to take his chiefs and advance party this a.m. so
Yuenter went and Swelt squeezed in. Those two aren't back yet so they must have
really taken in the town.*

*Well with the 1st boat about 20 sailors on shore leave and the brass with a
couple of nurses went I oozed up to the head of the gang plank to look over as
they left and an LCVP (Higgins boat) loaded with cargo came along side. The
Naval officer motioned for the men to come down — some officers of 308th were*

going ashore with their equipment. I managed to get caught in the middle and had a nice boat ride. Others who tried it in the next boat load were stopped. The first boat went to Kure. The one I was on loaded with C cargo went to the Naval Academy — on an island off Kure where the 308th is to set up. The trip was magnificent and a day I'll long remember.

It was 8:30 a.m. — clear and fresh the water was almost smooth. The low rising sun shone brightly on the slopes — green with trees and terraced gardens. It's really invigorating to get out of that humid tropical heat anyway one feels like living again.

On the trip in we passed dozens of American ships again and came fairly close to the sunken Jap battleship I told you about in my first letter. Really not much to see but a hulk of rusty iron. From our ship it must have been 3 to 4 miles to a small inlet or channel where we came within about 100 feet of shore and could really see things. Could see people walking, riding bicycles etc., but mostly sitting around it seemed. There was one long low brick building constructed to get the maximum benefit from the sun but for the most part the houses were a mess. I'm speaking of a small village along the shore. It seems that all the villages here are of necessity along the shore with the mountains rising steeply above their back door if they have any. And it appears that all the people around here live in villages.

The houses are built on these steep slopes clear down to and over the water's edge. They are packed tightly together with only an occasional alley between them. It resembles the hills of San Francisco in that respect but the houses are so much different. Most are just shacks although there were a few two or three story houses obviously holding several families so that they looked like large bird houses. Windows and doors if any were wide open. They were all unpainted and dingy but the insides were clean if bare from what I could see.

This little strait was only about 200 yds. wide. On the opposite side (Kure side) from the houses I described, were a sandy beach where a few men squatted on their haunches in typical Japanese fashion and fished with throw lines. An occasional woman walked along with a basket on her head. I think that practice probably helps account for the short spaced steps of the Jap women. They never stride out as American women.

Beyond these short but narrow straits the sea widened out into a big bay. (This is all the Inland Sea.) Here were many small boats with men fishing from them all using drop lines. They seemed quite active about it, but I didn't see any fish.

This widened expanse of water has Kure on one side and the Naval Academy on the other, maybe this drawing will help. In this big bay we counted 3 more sunken Jap battle ships all close to shore. I got a picture of one fairly close, all rusty and still covered with camouflage nets. There were 2 carriers there also which seemed quite intact. I'm beginning to understand what became of the Jap fleet. They were of course bombed as our fleet never got in here till after the armistice. We can really thank the air corps for a lot. It would seem like a hopeless task to invade this place 120 miles of island locked straits and all of the land steep mountains that would have made us pay dearly with our soldiers. I'm truly thankful an invasion was not needed.

We passed many small fishing boats 25 — 50 feet long — all wood — rough and unpainted, bobbing about like corks. They hardly seemed capable of keeping afloat themselves and yet I saw one loaded high with a family and all its worldly possessions it seemed. Some of them have motors, inboard and some both motors and sails. The sails are square or quadrangular — hard to describe. I think I have a good picture of one. Some of the smaller boats are powered by a single large oar or sweep in the stern which one or two men "wiggle" back and forth. It's fantastic, but they move.

Our boat dropped us on a small dock which is apparently the pier for the village ferry which arrived from the mainland about then. A cute little craft which resembles a miniature Mississippi River Show Boat — and it was really loaded.

A little way from the dock was the gates of the Jap Naval Warehouses, with guards. There was a nice Jap built bus there driven by a G.I. which took us to the other side of the island to the Naval Academy. I'd guess it was at least 2 miles. The water on the academy side of the island is said to be too heavily mined for traffic yet. Incidentally we had seen 3 mine sweepers at work on the way in.

The bus was relatively new, newer than any I had ridden on in the states since the war started. It had a right hand drive and we drove on the left hand side of this road — or street — as it was lined with a double row of houses all the way. It was a dirt road with open gutters on both sides. Much of it was fairly deeply cut in the hillsides.

All Jap traffic was on foot or bicycles. Most of the men were in uniform or parts of one as were the boys. Many of the men walked arm in arm with women or woman and children and carried a valise. I have a hunch they were just returning from the war. Ironical isn't it, we win and get stuck here 8,000 miles from home.

The Japs must have a terrific birth rate. The place was lousy with kids. If one was old enough to walk alone he or she usually had a baby strapped on her back. It's a slick trick too. I'll show you how it's done with a single figure of 8 when I get home — provided Suzanne isn't too big.

The people are clean and friendly for the most part. One little girl said, "Good Morning" and smiled proudly. The kids wear no shoes only sandals like I sent you. The women wear wooden "platform" shoes. The men wear mostly rubber soled, two toed shoes.

We were dropped at a big building in the academy — I understand this corresponds to our Annapolis. This is to be the home of the 308th General Hospital. It must have been a beautiful place in its prime but it looks as though it had been abandoned for many months. However they say it was used until after their defeat.

The first building which is to be used as living quarters and probably for at least part of the hospital is a huge 3 story building built quadrangular with a large court in the center with gardens and pools.

Entryways were on all four sides with broad cement steps and wide corridors. There were no doors except into the rooms so apparently the weather is never too cold. There is also no apparent means of heating the room — and they were cold.

Many windows were out and the rooms were in disorder. They were large class rooms much like any American schools. Most of the equipment had been thrown out including the straw mattresses. It should make a nice hospital if they can keep warm. This building faced by the parade which had grown considerably to weeds. The whole campus is on the water's edge. There was a big ship and several smaller boats apparently used for training purposes nearby.

There were many other buildings. The most pretentious one I visited. Had huge pillars in front and wide stone steps like a State Capitol. It was the museum and most of the rooms were bare. Either the Japs stole a march on us or the GI souvenir hunters are very active. Or maybe we just wanted the building. The rooms were huge and the walls "marbleized". About the only interesting thing there was "The Emperors Room" a small furnished dining room, very antique, apparently belonging to some ancient big shot.

The Gymnasium was a large building with cars, a lot of them in a warehouse, and I doubt that they will all be running soon. They look like an Austin and appear very top heavy with their narrow treads. There was a nice Buick Sedan whizzing around also of about 1938 vintage, which the boys had worked a whole day to get in running order.

Many of the buildings were marked off-limits so one of the soldiers told me I'd better hurry and help myself if I wanted any souvenirs before the MPs took over. He took me in a warehouse and gave me a swell ships clock which I didn't take because it was too big to manage. There were a lot of other instruments there that meant very little to me, including various guns for shooting flares and life lines. Most of the stuff looked obsolete to my inexperienced and prejudiced eyes.

I picked up a bugle with braids and I'll try to bring it home to the best musician in the Thayer family, who will get it? Also got a couple of small rubber weather balloons.

By this time it was 11 o'clock so I went into the mess hall and ate C Rations with the boys and drank water brought from Tinian we don't trust the Jap water yet. The huge kitchen had two batteries of huge iron kettles heated by steam (about 6 – 8 each) and about 4 ft in diameter. They told me they were for cooking rice. There were 3 ranges, smaller than an army range to do the rest of the cooking.

The plumbing in the dorm was interesting. No wash bowls but a long trough with faucets about every 2 feet. In another large room were rows of urinals and along each wall the rows of little "salon" doors. The surprise to me came when I looked in. The bowls here were flush with the floor. Nice shiny white porcelain shaped like a rectangular bird bath with pull chain. Flush boxes above. May I again refer you to the Japanese position of squatting mentioned earlier in the letter. Proctologists have told me it's a very healthy and effective position.

We hitch hiked a ride back to the dock on a truck. The absence of stores struck me on the way back. At least I didn't see anything that looked like a store to me. There was no boat ready to go back so I browsed through the naval warehouses along the shore. They were of flimsy construction with sheet iron roofs. Many of the wooden supports were mortared together and held with a wooden pin in place of nails. There were a few bomb hats but no fire damage here. One warehouse was packed with bombs, torpedoes and a few mines. A narrow gauge railway wandered around the place. There were numerous bomb cellars dug here and there and all buildings were camouflaged with paint.

The return trip took us closer to Kure and I could see the skeleton of a huge plant apparently a ship yard, which was still smoking heavily. Some of the boys who were in Kure today said the entire business district is burned out.

The empty boat splashed around plenty with the return trip and there was plenty of spray. No one searched me when I got on board and I got back as the boys were cleaning up after dinner. So I got some ice cream.

Someone just handed me a copy of regulations about conduct ashore and it appears I may have been a bit indiscreet.

From all I've heard and seen this place shouldn't be too bad. The people are civil enough, the soldiers salute very respectfully.

If this is a sample of Japan I don't see how they ever expected to win a war. Their equipment is so inadequate and their resources so meager. However I can understand their feeling of need for expansion much more reasonably than the Germans. Offhand I'd say the only thing the Japanese excel us in is in reproduction, which seems to have gone on unimpeded.

After seeing how they lived in the two villages I saw, I guess our treatment of the interned Japs at Camp Churo on Tinian was not to be criticized.

Rumor hath it that we will depart Tuesday for our destination which takes about 1 ½ days. Our advance party left by train from Kure tonight. There is a tunnel between Kuyushu and Honshu I hear.

Church was to have been this a.m. at 10 but was postponed because of the noise of winches till this afternoon. Bill preached but could hardly be heard above the noise.

He and Ray are writing down here in their ward room too and there is a bridge game waiting for me. I played all yesterday afternoon and this afternoon too. We sit on the floor of a gun turret where it's fairly clean, out of the way and not too windy.

It's a heck of a way to kill time, but there is so much of it to kill that we do just about everything. No one thought we'd be here long or we might have had some medical books to read.

Love to you all,
Dad

You blew yourself to rugs for an anniversary present so I bought a pipe today $5.25 at ships' store. Looks good too.

I took a few pictures today so please save this letter for me to help identify them when I get home.

You suggested I write a letter for Ma Almen [editor of the Truman Tribune]. Ask her if she approves this one? If you interpret it for her. Also since it's a literary masterpiece send it on to mother.

They say there has been no mail here since the Navy got here 6 weeks ago.

10/29/45 — Nearly thru unloading—will probably sail tomorrow.

10/30/45 — Started for Sasebo this AM beautiful thru the Inland Sea — but by 4 PM we hit the Pacific & it really was the roughest I've seen. The ship rolled & pitched violently & I was sick similarly. However before midnight we had entered the East China Sea & it was smooth. So I enjoyed a good breakfast after 14 hrs. in bed.

10/31/45 — Anchored about noon just outside the harbor of Sasebo & the CO went ashore. We were expected but there is no place for us so we will have to await orders for a few days.

11/05/45 — We moved into harbor & anchored the next day. Where we have since sat. Life aboard ship hasn't been too bad. We have moved up to the #1 compartment & nurses back to dormitory. A few have been going ashore to look around.

Cruiser *Montpelier* in Sasebo Anchorage.

Our reconnaissance party came back from Fukuoka last night to report that we are going in to the post office Bldg there which already has 2 Sta & 1 Gen Hospitals living there. We are to go there by train Wed 7 Nov.

11/07/45 Wednesday — went ashore in L.C.V.P. waited an hour for marine trucks to take us to Station where we waited another hour before our special train arrived. All 3rd class Jap coaches 13 of them. Ate our K rations & left about 12:30. Had a very interesting trip thru grader tunnels & then thru a broad valley of rice fields & small villages. With an occasional bombed city. About 4:30 arrived in Fukuoka — at a nice station. Then in trucks thru the city to our hospital bldg. — in the Postal Ins. Bldg. located on edge of a park with a lagoon — very pretty. A main street with street car line & bus runs by the front. The bldg. is 10 yrs old. Concrete construction, 4 stories, covering over a block & with a huge open area in center. There is no heating but has lights & running water — cold & forbidden to drink. Across the street & around all has been bombed out. The 123 Sta Hosp in the bldg. gave us hot supper & fed us next day. Then the 309th took over.

11/08/45 Thursday — Walked thru the park & saw some nice residences across the lake. In afternoon walked thru some of the shops near the hospital. Played bridge in evening.

Arriving in Kure.

11/09/45 Friday — This AM went up town by hitch hiking & walking. 90% of area is bombed out. Got $40 changed to yen. 600 Went thru a Dept. Store most of which was occupied by officers — Very little to sell — Got some pens in a stationery store. This PM really goofed off. Rode a trolley to end of line — walked & rode a truck 20 miles thru rice fields & little villages. Wandered about. Tried to get a kimono without success, bought a pretty comb. Some of the trip was along coast — very beautiful — much like California with Pine trees, rock, & sandy beach. Officers club had beer & Jap beer tonite. I tasted the latter — I believe I'd prefer it to many American beers.

11/14/45 Wednesday — Still freezing in this big barn. Have little kerosene heaters, no equipment, however we have opened a 10 bed male ward & 6 bed female ward of which I am chief.

Had one letter from home since arrival. Things look very discouraging. Administration of this organization is exceedingly stupid. Yesterday our 15th wedding anniversary was spent quietly as far apart as humanly possible — I'm sure I shall long remember the momentous occasion.

11/16/45 Friday — Today really was a day to remember. 3 of us went to the Imperial Fukuoka U. Med. School which escaped bombing. Were introduced by Prof of Med to Surgical Prof, who gave us a student to show us around. Watched an appendectomy, went thru a women's surgical ward. Went thru the old Anatomy bldg., Physiology & Biochemistry bldg., & the new Biology Bldg. All equipment was old and obsolete — books & Xray all old. The students were very anxious to learn & anxious to please us. Want us to come back Mon for gastric resection.

This town was bombed June 19th by 60 B-29s Only one raid & this town of 330,000 is now 270,000. 2,000 died and the remainder have been segregated elsewhere.

This PM bought a parasol & shopping baskets.

11/19/45 Monday — Last week I opened two wards — a men's ward & female ward then surrendered the male ward to Capt. McDonald. Today surrendered the female ward to Surgery as a recovery ward and have to open 2 new wards (women's & officers) but have 2 ward officers. Today we received 32 patients, transfers from marine hospital which is closing down. It had a nice steam heated building & we bring these patients — most of them sick — into this big unheated barn — all to satisfy the ego of one man at the peak of his career after seventeen years in the army. I hate to think of compulsory military training for 1 year for my boys to subject them to a year of such stupidity as can only be found in the army. The same routine continues day after day — kill time. All day, play bridge in the evening.

Have started a class in Japanese language.

11/28/45 Wednesday — Business is good, more patients (170) than we have room for with all the help occupying the building. We have 27 new nurses from the 13 GH & a colored laundry unit. Assisted at my first laparotomy in 7 mo. yesterday turned out to be a liver abscess.

Went thru a Jap airplane factory today — light bomber (Bettys) saw plenty of tanks guns & ammunition. Bought Suzie a kimono. Have done little work but have looked over the town & surroundings pretty well. Got my first letter on APO 929 today — mailed the 16th.

12/01/45 Saturday — Still doing the same. Evacuated 1st plane load of patients to Nagaya today. Have about 170 patients and 800+ personnel. Really cold today and there is no way to keep warm. This afternoon Baurland and I went to the U. & went thru the Orthopedic bldg. Saw their equipment & wards. Nice big modern type bldg. but run down and dirty. One doctor spoke English fair and we went on ward rounds with a whole group. Saw a lot of interesting stuff. They were treating fractures — with 1 femur with traction only, because they have no Smith Peterson nails which they formerly used. Some fellow had invented a hip exerciser of which they were quite proud. The Prof of Orthopedics is said to be the best in Japan. There was a large "Sanatorium" of bone tbc — Potts disease, one with tbc of pubis. Several open reduction with wiring — very good, no screws. Several on leg bone grafts. One Veteran of Korean Campaign with re-fracture of femur, injured in August. Several plastic surgery repairs of burns from June 19th B-29 raid. One child with pedicle graft from belly to hand. They are very proud of their sutures made of strands of palm leaves. There were 2 spinal cord tumors. Their charts are remarkable for completeness, diagnosis in German. Neurological marked out on chart — photomicrograph of tissue and photo of specimen with neurological charts showing recovery. X-ray pictures are really small — charts all 10x12 pictures are very poor quality.

12/15/45 — Went on another trip with Bill, Joe, & Bob into this rural area, saw some very beautiful valleys of terraced rice and wheat fields, and small orange orchards. It was the prettiest part of Japan I've seen. Got back to hospital at 5 PM to find that Dr Marotomi had been waiting for me for 2 hours. He is 2nd associate Professor of Orthopedics. We showed him what orthopedics cases we had and then got him a tray on the ward and ate with him in the ward office. Then visited in our quarters. Has had his job 8 years, is full time. Has a wife and (1) 4 mos. old baby. Told of the one atomic bomb case he had followed. Described

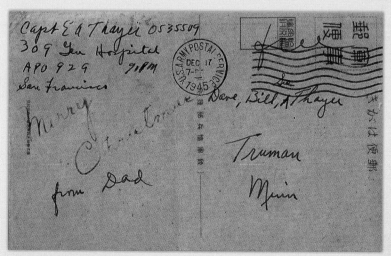

Christmas postcard Mike sent to his children from Japan.

113

practice of (their) medicine. All OB is done in homes by midwives except few wealthy who go to the U. Private doctors are surgeons with their own small hospital or only a "dispensary". There is one small municipal hospital and also a contagious disease hospital which was all bombed out. It was a very interesting visit and he left around 8.

Reynolds, Lichterman and I then went to a "high class" Geisha[11] house and browsed around for a couple of hours and so another day in Japan.

11. This definition of a geisha is taken from a handout given to U.S. servicemen during the war, describing the four classes of the women of Japan. Japan had about 30,000 Geisha girls who were selected at age 9 or 10 to be groomed for this profession. The parents were paid a good sum of money and the child was educated to sing, dance, and serve tea according to the ceremonial way, to make bouquets, to make embroidery, to chatter in a pleasant manner, even to write short poetry, to play koto or shamisen (two Japanese musical instruments). When she is of age she will go to private families to sing, dance, or play for the entertainment of some distinguished guest. By profession she is a singer and a dancer, an artist, and as such she has much freedom of talk and action. She boasts of the fact that she is not a prostitute. Many Japanese love stories center about Geisha girls marrying a rich admirer for whom she had previously entertained.

12/18/45 Tuesday — Two days of cold rain and today snow. The NW wind off the bay has put out the fires so it is freezing and last nite the lites went off at 10 and stayed off till 6 because of the storm.

We now have hospital beds and mattresses to sleep on.

Sunday P.M. made my 2nd trip to a certain dry goods wholesaler and he gave us several silk "presentos" and we are to go back with presents (of candy and tooth brushes).

This PM I went alone to a private hospital up the street which I had heard an American educated doctor owned. He took me in his office and gave me tea. Then I took off my shoes and went thru his hospital and finally he took me into his home and gave me beer and canned corn beef. His only daughter died 2 months ago of tbc and the son in law is studying surgery at the U. His son is studying med in Tokyo. His wife spoke English even better than he. She was born in Hawaii. He, Dr. T Tanamachi came to U.S. at age 16 in 1910 took up med at Chicago Univ and post grad at the U of Tenn in 1921 practiced in Portland Oregon. He does only surgery. Hospital holds 21 patients. They bring their own bedding and food and a relative to take care of them. Fares are 4-6-8-or 10 yen a day. His fee is 150 Yen for appendectomy. He also does brain surgery. Has deep Xray therapy but machine was broken in moving it in to bomb shelter. Has good equipment — mostly American except Xray. Bldg is run down some because as he says they did not paint because of danger of losing it in bombing anyways. His bomb shelter of concrete was built 4 years ago. Had a water tank constructed on roof, fear bombing, also had all patients in shelter at time of bombing. Building in 2 stories and private home looks like brick. Patients are referred in. He also varies his fees with patient's ability to pay. I promised to come back and bring him tobacco and cigarettes and he said he would invite me for sukiyaki.

12/20/45 — This evening went out to see a "high class" restaurant but were refused admission because M.P.s do not approve, prices too high. Wandered into another Jap bath house and caused consternation. Tasted some bulk Jap whiskey, which brought back memories of prohibition.

Went back to a dumpy little shop and bought a vase I had seen in the forenoon trip 40 yen, I got it for 20 yen and 1 package of cigarettes.

12/21/45 — Examined an American woman, wife of a Jap, who has been here since 41. She is a native of Kansas and she and her husband had a business in Chicago for 15 yrs. For 1st 2 yrs of war all went well, then her husband went south to Shanghai to ask an interpreter. Message came back in official Japanese which she just got interpreted yesterday. He went to Siam, had operation on legs and was being sent back to Japan when his boat was sunk. She has a vitamin deficiency B (riboflavin) probably, sore tongue, dry itchy cracked skin. Has lived on rice and potatoes for 4 years with some bread the first 2 yrs, no fruits or vegetables because they caused diarrhea.

12/25/45 — Merry Christmas "Chresemus Omedeta" This is one I'll remember a long time.

We were free from noon 24th to 26th except for necessary work. So yesterday Casey and I stopped at Dr. Tanamachis. I gave him some tobacco and asked him if he would get me some sake. He invited us in and brought out sake, which we drank cold. Also a shot of gin, we drank a quart when he gave the rest to some M.P.s. Then he took us down town in his 41 Chev to the tax commissioner and got a permit to get some Sake. Then we went and got 3 ½ gal. bottles. He gave one each to Casey and I, and took us back to hospital. In front of Motor Pool it stalled and we got gas for him and found a wire off his coil. He wanted us back for 8 P.M. Casey was a little high and went to bed.

7 PM the choir had a service very good too followed by a party in the rec hall. Brandy punch and we received our qm ration — candy bars, carton cig and 5 cigars, can of grape fruit juice and peanuts.

Then the Red Cross had a package for each — candy etc.

Then this A.M. the nurses gave me a Xmas present — 2 sets of GI drawers with a cute note.

About 8:30 last night I took Lichterman and Hammer to Dr. Tanamachis. He introduced us to a Judge and Assistant Attorney General and we went to Geisha house where we were fed scrumptious steak, sweet potatoes, boiled fish, greens, and plenty of hot sake. The girls entertained and it was an experience to remember.

This AM went to church, short service. Had to think that the folks were enjoying Christmas Eve about that time.

12/28/45 — Last night Dr. Tanamachi took us to Judge Nakamuras home for dinner, (Lichterman, Hammer, Bourland). Six course dinner of Jap dishes, hot sake and beer lasting 3 hours or more. My application for release came back 26th so started it over again but there is little hope.

12/31/45 — Started out in the 309th Club and gravitated to Fukuoka Officers Club from which Lichterman and I returned in time for the passage of the old year.

01/01/46 — Big dinner of Turkey and trimmings, very good too. Took a walk in afternoon and the streets were full of Japs on their way to visit their shrines, beautifully dressed, took a lot of pictures. Also the C.O.s tea and reception at the club.

In the evening following the Japanese custom Boukland and I went to call on our friend Dr. Tanamachi with a present. Had sake, steaks, with him and later on the Judge and a couple attorneys came in so it was quite an evening. Later Bob, Lichterman and I went out for a walk, ended up with police escorts very interesting.

01/04/46 — This PM Lichterman and Reynolds took me for tea to the richest Jap in the city who owns 47 homes and is in the steel business. Had a ceremonial tea by his wife, "very interesting".

01/08/46 — Lichterman, Reynolds, and I called on Dr. Tanamachi and after seeing a patient with him we had whiskey, sake, Peanuts, and steak and a very nice gab fest, Mrs T spent her time with us contrary to usual custom.

01/09/46 — Bourland and I joined a party of 8 other officers and Dr. T on a dinner party to Mr. Nakoshima, a most beautiful home and banquet followed by dancing with daughters and Geisha girls. Son and daughter in law from Tokyo were very nice have two baby girls. Got home at 1 AM.

01/24/46 — Went to Univ this AM to see a gastrectomy. Saw a class room with many pathological specimens and pretty xrays of venograms and arteriograms, etc. Prof Tomada operated. 8 yrs ago he visited Mt Sinai and Mayo Clinic. He gave us clinical history on this 56 yr old male with distress since Nov. Under spinal, metycaine, he did at Belfour type subtotal gastrectomy — using silk all the way and ending with an entero enterostomy after an anterior anastomosis. Very Fast and good. Scrub nurse excellent. Teamwork beautiful. Asepsis questionable.

01/27/46 — Took a drive thru the country with Ackerman. Muddy roads, coal mines, small shops.

Starting my second year with 309th. Bourland got orders to a Dispensary today. Have just finished a week of surgical call and 2 ODs some surgery.

02/04/46 — Got my radio gram emergency leave.

02/05/46 — Turned over my duties and property. Got clearance and at 5:17 PM left Fukuoka. Got a Pullman, lower berth about 8:30 and had a fair night's sleep.

Every city we went thru was badly burned and bombed out. Plenty of empty factories in fact it seems they are all either destroyed or idle. The same meager living conditions seem to exist all thru Japan. Houshu looks just like Knyushu.

The train made pretty good time and arrived at Okasake about 4 PM 6 Feb where we got on trucks and rode 7 miles to 11th Repl Depot.

Processing started at once and I got to my quarters about 7 pm too late for supper — but got a lunch at 7:30. Had chocolate and a cheese sandwich.

02/07/46 — Mermac wave is loading today but I guess I won't make it. The Altoona Victory is here also and starts loading in a day or so so I'll possibly get that and probably in troop compartment.

5 PM I was notified that I leave here at 10:30 PM for Tokyo to take a plane home — Happy Day —

I'll probably be sick but no worse than the hold of a Victory ship and I hope a little faster.

Left the 11th Repl Dep at 11:30 pm 7 Feb. and went to Okasake station where train was very late. Left at 1:30 A.M. sat up in day couch but slept in sleeping bag which I shared with an E~

Got to Tokyo about 9 AM and got a jeep to take us to A.T.C. headquarters where we were billeted. No planes left Thur or Fri (8 & 9th) and Sat & Sun were full. So I had a chance to see Tokyo. Rained the 8th preceded by snow so Tokyo was white when we arrived. Checked luggage with customs and weighed in Thu

PM (8th). Walked around a bit down the Ginsa with its sidewalk markets and thru a Dept. store. Show in the evening in a Jap Theater.

02/09/46 Saturday — walked extensively Tour the Emperors Park and business district of Tokyo where buildings are modern and undamaged because they surround the palace — which is itself surrounded by a series of 6 moats.

In P.M. took a sight-seeing trip around the city. Buildings that remain are modern day structures. The new Diet bldg. is very western.

American and British Embassy are intact.

Went thru the Meiji Memorial Bldg with its 80 paintings. Memorial to Emperor Meiji, grandfather of present emperor.

Wandered thru the Imperial theater. Went to show at night.

02/10/46 Sunday — Went to church in Dai ichi Bldg (McArthurs Bldg) took a walk — found the Officers Red Cross Club.

In P.M. went to concert in Hibiya Hall by the Nypon Philharmonica Orchestra, Joseph Rosenstone conducting. It was pretty grand.

In evening went to same place to see USO "What a Life" with Henry Aldrich followed by a movie the Dally Sisters.

Tokyo is so far ahead of the rest of Japan there is no comparison.

ATC where I stayed is a modern 7 story Bldg next to Dai Ichi bldg. and across street from Palace grounds. The food was good. Served by Jap waitresses on a table cloth, silver, china and flowers on each table.

02/11/46 Monday — Walked and walked. Sold my watch for 1,200 Y ($80) and bought an obi for 270 Y plus 2 pkg cigarettes.

Got a small silk Kimono for Sue also.

Left Tokyo about 4 PM by bus for Atsugi Air Port (1 ½ hr ride). Took off at

7 PM for Guam — air 8 ½ hr ride. We were fortunate to get a C54 with plush seats. Had smooth flying all the time. Arrived Guam 5:00 AM and went to bed till 7 and got up for breakfast. Guam was hot and sultry. Called Betty King at 123 Fleet Hospital. Took off from Guam at 1PM Tue 12th in another plush seat job — and arrived 8 ½ hrs later at Kwajalein 12:20 am 13 Feb stopped 1 hr. left Kwajalein 1:30 AM 13 Feb flew 8 ½ hrs and landed at Johnston Island 11:50 AM.

02/12/46 — this is strange little dry hot spot in the broad Pacific ¼ sq mile with a runway 1 mile long. Had a good dinner and left at 1 P.M. Flew for 4 ½ hrs and arrived at Hickan Field Hawaii 5:30 PM Tues 12 Feb.

Hawaii looked beautiful and green from the air. The beach was lovely. We passed Customs officials and now have our luggage again. Had a shower, shave etc and was too late for supper so 4 of us went to Honolulu. I had a couple of drinks (martinis) at Alexander Young Hotel. Took a cab to Waikiki and had a swell steak dinner at P.Y. Chongs. Everything closes about 10:30 or 11 so we came back by cab (12 mi) and to bed.

May get a plane out tonight — Wed 13 Feb 46

Map showing where Mike was stationed in Fukuoka, Japan, between Hiroshima and Nagasake.

Village on the straits near Kure.

Local children on the dock at Kure.

Japanese village in the narrow straits approaching Kure.

Japanese Naval Academy near Kure, the location of the 308th. Small truck and naval guns are seen in the foreground.

Sunken and camouflaged Japanese battle ship, opposite Kure. This is the island on which the 308th set up. A Japanese ferry is in the foreground. Note the terraced hills.

City destroyed by bomb.

Fukuoka and harbor from the same hill and shrine that showed the lake and hospital. The dock area is flattened. Hospital is to the right.

Fukuoka waterfront in January 1946. The name of the boat is *The Little King O. Sasebo*.

At the waterfront with reconstruction in progress in the background.

Reconstruction efforts.

Reconstruction efforts.

The 309th General Hospital from Ohori Park.

The lake and island from the roof of the hospital. This is Ohori Park.

Typical entrance to a
Japanese home.

Wrecked Japanese seaplanes at a base near Fukuoka.

Main street of Fukuoka. Mike took this especially to show the woman carrying baskets and child and leading two others.

Ox and "Honey Wagon" in town near Fukuoka. They really stunk. [Honey wagon refers to a wagon used to collect manure]

New Year's Day 1946, very beautiful Kimonos.

Cable street car was one form of transportation.

Entrance to shrine.
Trout is the name of
the man in the photo.

Two geisha girls and Mama San on New Year's Day 1946.

Reynolds, Thayer, Trout, McDonald, and Heron on New Year's Day 1946 with geisha girls.

Geisha girl postcard.

Military personnel going down a street in Fukuoka.

New Year's Day 1946. Japanese merchants and wife.

Train station

Transportation

11th Replacement Depot.

Tokyo

Emperor's Palace grounds.

Postcard of entrance to prefecture that Mike sent to the family.

The main street uptown from the hospital in Fukuoka. Mostly all ruins except for concrete skeletons.

Ruined buildings in town of Harbor. Sugar factory in foreground.

January 1946 on the Fukuoka waterfront. Mike is learning about a local farming technique.

309th General Hospital with Thayer, Bourland, and Wandke.

Mike wrote on the back of this postcard: "The bridge is the only recognizable structure."

Post card of an island in Ohori park.

Inside the envelope was a list of Japanese words and their English translations.

Post card sent from Japan.

The time for war is done and now let us find peace.

戦争の時間行われ、今では平和 つを見 けることができます。

— *Dr. Mike Thayer*

The atom bomb was no 'great decision.'
It was merely another powerful weapon in the arsenal of righteousness.

— *Harry S. Truman*

The use of the atomic bomb, with its indiscriminate
killing of women and children, revolts my soul.

— *Herbert Hoover*

I call upon the scientific community in our country, those who gave us nuclear weapons,
to turn their great talents now to the cause of mankind and world peace, to give
us the means of rendering those nuclear weapons impotent and obsolete.

— *Ronald Reagan*

National Address on March 23, 1983,

concerning his proposed Strategic Defense Initiative, later to be known as 'Star Wars.'

Retiring president of the Minnesota Academy of General Practice, "Bill" Watson, hands over gavel to incoming President "Mike" Thayer (left).

12

CONTINUING PRACTICE AFTER THE WAR

Mike's last day of service was April 5, 1946. After returning home to Truman, he continued his practice there for six more months. He was required to use the hospital in Fairmont because he had closed the one in Truman before leaving for the war. The Truman Commercial Club offered to build him a hospital in Truman, but he did not want the responsibility of working around the clock that managing a hospital required.

Mike moved to Fairmont, a 20-minute drive from Truman, so he could practice in a hospital managed by another doctor. He began his practice there on September 2, 1946 with Dr. Joe Wandke from Chicago, his good friend whom he had met in the service. Dr. Wandke was

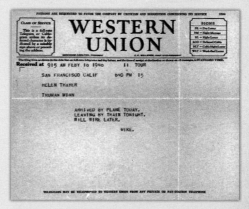

Coming-home telegram

the orthopedics specialist. Later they invited Dr. George Kramer, a Mankato surgeon, to join them. Mike served as the family practitioner and performed minor surgeries for the clinic.

Dr. Thayer disliked socialized medicine and believed no patient should ever be turned away because of inability to pay. He also believed the extra pay of specialists was undeserved because his own training was very intense and broad, covering all areas. He helped found the Minnesota Academy of General Practice in 1946—now the Minnesota Academy of Family Physicians —and was a lifetime member. He also served as the academy's treasurer and president.

Strolling 1

June 13, 1946

On Friday morning, the doors of the new *Red Owl Agency Food Store*, owned by Barlow Bros. were open to the buying public of the community. The new Red Owl Agency Food Store is located in the D.R. Peterson building next door to the *Rialto Theatre.*

LaVerna (Breitbarth) Hiatt passed away at a Fairmont Hospital Monday afternoon after giving birth to a healthy son, Verle Dean. The 27-year-old had been hospitalized since June 6 with a serious kidney infection. Thursday evening Mrs. Don Peterson was honored guests at a pink and blue shower with Mrs. Don Huemoeller and Mrs. Rollo Larsen as hostesses.

Mrs. Wm. Hoelmer is improving nicely from her recently operation and was able to return home. Her daughter, Mrs. Kenneth Halverson, is caring for her. Mrs. Carl Saucke and son, Donald, flew to Truman from Farnhamville, IA Sunday to spend the day with relatives, the Herman Gollwitzers and the Ernest Borcherts. Donald Saucke was a flyer during the war and is now an instructor at Armstrong, IA.

Going Fishing! During the past three years I got a little behind in my fishing, so I'm going to catch up in the next ten days. My office will be closed from the 10th through the 25th of June. *E.A. Thayer*. The Carl Amelon children, Roland, Lawrence, Maynard and Ruth of Centralia, MO are visiting Truman relatives. They are staying with their grandparents, Mrms. Henry Ritz.

Truman Tribune, June 13, 1946.

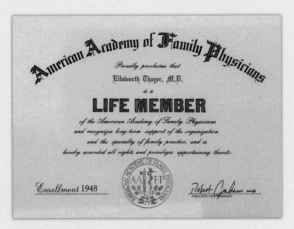

American Academy of Family Physicians
Dr. Thayer became a lifetime member of the American Academy of Family Physicians in 1948. He was very active in the organization.

November-December

Medical Diggings

President Ellsworth & Helen Thayer

Official Publication of the

Minnesota Academy of General Practice

"Minnesota's Family Physicians"

President Ellsworth Thayer and wife Helen on the cover of *Medical Diggings*.

STATE OFFICERS
MINNESOTA ACADEMY
OF
GENERAL PRACTICE

President
ELLSWORTH THAYER, M.D.
Fairmont

President-Elect
HERB HUFFINGTON, M.D.
Waterville

Vice-President
EDWIN A. KILBRIDE, M.D.
Worthington

Secretary-Treasurer
HENRY W. QUIST, M.D.
Minneapolis

Executive Secretary
MISS DARLENE COMSTOCK
123 So. Second St.
Waterville

Speaker
EDWARD W. CIRIACY, M.D.
Ely

Vice-Speaker
JOHN W. ANDERSON, M.D.
Blue Earth

DELEGATES TO AAGP
CONGRESS

R. O. QUELLO, M.D.
Minneapolis

JAMES A. COSGRIFF, JR., M.D.
Olivia

ALTERNATES TO AAGP

HERB HUFFINGTON, M.D.
Waterville

R. B. POTTER, M.D.
Minneapolis

November-December, 1964

Medical Diggings

Official Publication of the
Minnesota Academy of General Practice

Published Bimonthly

Vol. 19, No. 6 _____ November - December

Contents

President's Message _____ Page 4
Board of Directors _____ Page 6
Refresher Pictures _____ Page 8-12
Dr. Cosgriff's Address _____ Page 14
Calendar _____ Page 19
Lederle Symposium _____ Page 20
CCOC Program _____ Page 21
Train to AAGP??? _____ Page 22

R. B. POTTER, M.D., *Editor*
3007 Nicollet Avenue
Minneapolis 8, Minn.

$2.00 *per year*
Subscription rates
from annual dues

Second-class postage
paid at Waterville,
Minnesota

Three

Retiring President 'Bill' Watson hands over the gavel to incoming President 'Mike' Thayer after the swearing in ceremony at the Annual Banquet September 16th. Following this Dr. Thayer receives his presidents key from Dr. Watson. This key used to be given to the president on retiring but last year the custom was changed so that the president would have it during his term of office.

Dr. Thayer's reputation was one of being a great doctor for delivering babies, although this was technically not his certified specialty. During his practice, he delivered over 3,000 babies. A patient for whom he had delivered 11 babies was promised that her 12th would be delivered for free, and he kept the promise. The family had one more child. When they had a family reunion in 1974, they invited Doc to their celebration, and the event made the local paper with the story about how he delivered all 13 children with the 12th for free.

Salics Entertain Doctor Who Delivered All of 13 Children

A BAKER'S DOZEN -- When the Ernest Salics of Nashville Township corraled all of their 13 children for a family doings a week ago, they invited Dr. E. A. Thayer of Fairmont, who had delivered all 13, to come. Mrms. Salic are in the left center of the picture. Doc Thayer is the white haired old guy in the right center. Mrs. Salic said "you never can tell" when the Tribune reporter asked her if there would be some more children.

Mrms. Ernest Salic, Sr., of Nashville, had all of thir 13 children at home for a family gathering on June 3 and they thoughtfully invited the family doctor who had delivered all of the 13.

Drms. E. A. Thayer of Fairmont, formerly of Truman, came for the event which was in celebration of the graduation of No. 7, (Lucinda) from the Granada–Huntley High School.

The Salics have a Winnebago address and attend St. Mary's Catholic Church in Winnebago.

"Somewhere along the line, Dr. Thayer asked me how many children I expected to have," said Mrs. Salic.

"I told him 'about a dozen' and he said when the 12th one came along he'd deliver it free -- and he did."

The Salic's brood ranges in age from 28 to 7 years. Mrs. Salic said she wasn't sure if there would be more.

They are: Claudine, now Mrs. Dale Meckes of Laury's Station, Pa.; Veronica; Ernest, Jr., married and living at Granada with one grandchild; Lawrence; Michael; Bonita, Lucinda; Peter; Dixie; Bing; Goria; Trina and Alicia.

Mrs. Salic, 45 years old, was the for-

mer Phyllis Vanora of Fairmont; Ernest, 53, was a son of Mrms. Joe Salic. It took a mere 14 chickens for the graduation party.

Cheaper By The Dozen!
The Fairmont Daily Sentinel

1995 — Salic Reunion.

Dr. Thayer was invited to celebrate the 50th wedding anniversary of Ernest and Phyllis Salic at their family farm with all thirteen children delivered by Dr. E.A. "Mike" Thayer surrounding him in this picture.

Another woman, Kathy Waldon Studer, tells the story of delivering Linda, her seventh child on Mother's Day, May 8, 1955. She was concerned for the family financially because her husband was unemployed and she did not know how she was going to support another child without any money. Dr. Thayer had delivered all seven of her children. After Linda's birth, Kathy waited for a bill that never came. When she called to find out about the bill, she was told that there was none. When asked about it, Dr. Thayer said, "This baby will be free because any mother who delivers on Mother's Day deserves a free one." Kathy always believed that Dr. Thayer forgave the charge because of her financial situation.

Kathy also talked about a time when she had Hepatitis and was hospitalized for two months. She was extremely ill. One night she was awakened in the middle of the night by Dr. Thayer massaging her feet and talking to her. She wondered why he would come in the middle of the night and spend so much time with her. In the morning a nurse told her that they had called Dr. Thayer to come because they did not think she would make it through the night. Massaging her feet and talking to her was one way to improve her circulation and keep her alive. It is great she is still alive to tell her story.

Kathy went on to have nine children. When the ninth one was born, Dr. Thayer's sense of humor showed when he and the nurse tried to guess how much it weighed by passing the baby back and forth and making a guess. Dr. Thayer said it would weigh over 11 lbs. and it weighed 11 lbs. 12 oz. At this point, he said, "If I had known that he was that much I could have cut off more umbilical cord to make the baby weigh less." Dr. Thayer always had a great sense of humor and bedside manner with the patients.

Kathy also recalled when one child became ill such as with chicken pox or whooping cough, she could not bundle them all up to take them into the doctor's office, so he made house calls. She says, "He was an awesome doctor who said all the right things. He would save free samples to give me because he knew I did not have extra money. He was more than a doctor; he was a friend." Kathy says she has been blessed with fifty grandchildren.

In 1971, Dr. Thayer helped found the Fairmont Medical Clinic to provide more medical specialists to the community and allow them to share on-call time. He himself appreciated the free time that sharing duties provided. He spent his with the family and enjoying his favorite pastimes of hunting, fishing, and gardening. His frugality never waned and he continued to record all revenue and expenses.

After Dr. Thayer retired in 1976, he kept his medical license current and saw to the healthcare needs of family and friends at retirement places in Arizona where he was a snow bird. When in Minnesota he returned to visit residents of the Lutheran Retirement home in Truman and at the Methodist Retirement home in Fairmont. He joked that most of his patients were in those homes so he would just go see them there. He also continued making house calls.

Four of the founders of the Fairmont Medical Clinic enjoying a watermelon break. Left to right: Dr. R.L. Zemke, Dr. E. A. Thayer, Dr. J.K. Gardner, Dr. E.E. Zemke.

PAULUS   BEECHER   MISS ANDERSON   MRS. HARTLEY   HARTLEY
DR. THAYER   DR. FEIGAL

Medical students greeted

Greeted at Interlaken Golf Club Saturday were medical students from the University of Minnesota who were weekend guests of the Medical Opportunities Committee of Fairmont Chamber of Commerce. Students John Beecher, his fiancee, Miss Janet Anderson and Mr. and Mrs. James Hartley are pictured here with Todd Paulus, C-C Ambassadors member and Drs. E.A. Thayer and William M. Feigal of the hospital staff. The visit was arranged by the Chamber committee to acquaint the students with advantages of a general rural practice. The students stayed with Fairmont doctors, were guests at a picnic Saturday afternoon and a dinner Saturday evening. They also sailed, boated and water skied on Fairmont's lakes, and went swimming at the Chain of Lakes Yacht Club. (Sentinel Photo by Bob Schroeder.)

Mike tried to promote the Fairmont area for new doctors to begin their practice.

The Thayer Boys

Mike in the middle, with the rest of the Thayer boys. He is holding his oldest grandson, Allen Thayer. On the left is Mike's son Bill holding Roger. Roger and Allen are both Bill's sons. David is on the right holding his son, Scott Thayer.

13

BLESSINGS OF CHILDREN, GRANDCHILDREN AND GREAT-GRANDCHILDREN

Mike delivered five of his ten grandchildren. Although some might think it strange that he delivered babies for his daughter and daughters-in-law, he provided care for all his children. Both of his daughters-in-law were from Truman and were Dr. Thayer's patients before they ever met his sons. Bill Thayer's wife, Elaine Williams, was herself delivered by Dr. Thayer, as were her brothers and sisters. So, it did not seem strange to go to a doctor who had been a family doctor.

Grandparent delivered twice within eight hours. A daughter, Susie Bakken (right) gave birth to a baby boy, Stephen; and a daughter-in-law, Edna Thayer (center) gave birth to a baby girl, Tamara. Both women shared the same room at the Fairmont Community hospital and had their babies delivered by Dr. Thayer. From *The Sentinel*, June 1, 1962, photo by Bob Schroeder.

Mike was the family doctor for his children and grandchildren. Roger Thayer remembers when the family would gather for a holiday or event that his grandpa would use that opportunity to get his grandchildren their annual physicals or immunizations. Sometimes they went to his office, and sometimes they were done right at home. He even pierced many granddaughters' ears. Granddaughter Tamara remembers one Christmas when she was in sixth grade and finally had permission from her mom to get her ears pierced. Her grandpa offered to take her to his office to get it done. Her cousins came with and one of them was teasing her saying there was a lot of blood squirting out. His face was really convincing as he looked at her ears with a horrified expression. Tamara fainted, and when her grandpa waved smelling salts in her face she woke up only to see her cousins laughing at her. Her ears were pierced without one drop of blood shed.

After Bill had a serious snowmobile accident, Mike X-rayed his son's dislocated shoulder and saw a portion of his lung in the X-ray that appeared black. Mike asked him to come in for more X-rays, and this time he had his nurse take the X-rays of his lungs (instead of his shoulder) to find and diagnose for his son that he had a black spot area on his lung that was highly suspicious of cancer. Mike referred Bill to the Mayo Clinic for surgery to see if the cancer could be removed. Mike watched his son's surgery from the observation area.

After the Mayo doctors cut into the lung area, they looked up at Mike and said, "I'm sorry Doc – there's nothing we can do." They closed Bill's incision area without removing anything. The cancer had spread too far. Bill was only 38 years old when he died, leaving behind a wife and three children. Diagnosing his own son's cancer was doubtless the most difficult thing Mike had ever done.

Mike and Helen surrounded by grandchildren: Allen, Kim, Roger, Steve, baby Jeni, Tamara and Scott.

Christmas 1971 was celebrated in Mike and Helen's home with all ten of their grandchildren. Those grandchildren are left to right: Roger Thayer, Scott Thayer holding his sister Brenda Thayer (by the tree), Steve Bakken holding his brother Doug Wright (in front), Kim Thayer holding Joni Wright, Tammy Thayer holding Jeni Wright, and kneeling in front of the tree, Allen Thayer.

Thayer annual Christmas celebration, ca. 1984. All ten grandchildren posed with their grandma and grandpa.

Special Celebrations

It was always wonderful to see Mike's niece, Barbara Tasa, and her family at the special Thayer get-togethers. Mike's sister Elizabeth had one child, Barbara. Mike's brother William had one child, Rosemary. Family was always very important to both Mike and Helen and they loved getting together.

Left to right: Helen Thayer, Curt and Barbara Tasa, and Mike Thayer.

Left to right: Mike, Jeremiah Thayer, Mason Espeseth (wearing a Santa hat), Allison Cooney, Emily Thayer standing behind great-grandma Helen, Helen holding Andrew Cooney, Katie Thayer, William Thayer sitting, Nathan Thayer standing on far right. Photo taken ca.1992.

Left to right: Will Thayer, Allison Cooney, great-grandpa Mike, Andrew Cooney, Molly Thayer, Ashley Thayer holding little sister Hannah Thayer, and great-grandma Helen. Photo taken ca. 1995.

Attending family events was very important to Mike and Helen. In the photo Mike is in the center of the Baptism of great-granddaughter Andrea Thayer on October 20, 1996. The family has great memories of celebrating Easter by attending church together followed by brunch at the Fairmont Country Club and maybe a round of golf. Cherished Christmas memories of a beautiful candle lit Christmas Eve church service was followed by Helen's homemade Christmas oyster stew or homemade vegetable beef soup. Santa Claus was always invited to their Christmas parties and managed to stop by on his busiest night to bring gifts and say hi to the children. One year the great-grandchildren were eagerly waiting to see if Santa would come down the chimney when he arrived for the party. While great-grandma Helen kept the kids busy in the kitchen with her delicious homemade almond cashew cookies and the Christmas sugar cookie cut outs beautifully decorated down to the

Great-granddaughter Andrea Thayer's Baptism.

ornate detail as they looked too pretty to eat, Mike made a fire in the fireplace. There came a knock on the front door and it was Santa. When the kids asked Santa why he did not use the chimney, Mike had to apologize to him because he was not thinking and had built a fire so it was too hot for Santa to come down. Every special birthday or big anniversary was celebrated with a party with the extended family. Helen was an excellent hostess, cook, and decorator to make these events even more special for the whole family.

The Thayers gathered to celebrate Helen's 90th birthday.

Mike and his oldest grandson, Allen Thayer.

Mike hunting on his farmland in Truman, Minnesota.

Mike had always enjoyed hunting with his children and passed on this tradition to his grand and great-grandchildren. He gave his oldest grandson, Allen, a 16-gauge shotgun for his first gun on his 15th or 16th birthday.

Pheasant hunting was always an important event for family and friends. It has been a tradition for the family to gather together every pheasant opener weekend for hunting on the family farms. This annual family tradition continues today on the opening pheasant hunting day with the families of Dr. Thayer's sons and daughter, which now includes grandchildren and great-grandchildren. Even for the non-hunters in the family, it is a fun reunion to gather and keep in touch. After hunting is over, the extended family gathers poolside at the Holiday Inn in Fairmont to have supper and swim. The hunting begins again Sunday morning.

Pheasant hunt, 1987
Left to right: Son-in-law Bill Wright, Mike, grandson Roger Thayer, and son David.

Mike and Helen brought lunch for the hunters and visited with them on their break. This was their last pheasant opener October, 2000. In the front row are great-grandsons William Thayer and Andrew Cooney. Sitting are Helen and Mike and kneeling to the left is grandson Allen Thayer. Standing in the back row are grandsons Roger Thayer and Doug Wright, great-grandson Jeremiah Thayer, and son David.

Pheasant hunting opening weekend, October 13, 2012. Back row, left to right: Doug Wright, Dave Thayer, Rachel Eisenschenk, Andrea Thayer, Mathew Eisenschenk, Keith Eisenschenk. Front row, left to right: Jeremiah Thayer, Nathan Thayer, Allen Thayer, William Thayer, William's fiancée Chelsea Erickson, Roger Thayer, 7 dogs, and 14 roosters shot!

Furthering the Legacy

Granddaughter Kim Thayer is the only direct descendant so far who has followed in his footsteps as a doctor. Dr. Kim Thayer, Urology Surgeon, lives in California with her husband and seven children.

While only one descendant has become a doctor, many more descendants have followed Dr. Thayer's patriotic example by serving their country in the military. Seeing his father proudly serve his country was one reason why David joined the service. This retirement photo was taken of Lt. Col. David Leroy Thayer after 27 years in the Air Force both active and reserves. Mike's grandson, Corporal Doug Wright, E4, served in the Marine Corps from 1989 to 1993 and served in the Gulf War. He was deployed to Okinawa, Japan, the Philippines, Tahiti, and Guam. Mike's great-grandson, Andrew Cooney, an E5 in the Seabees, is stationed in Gulfport, Mississippi. BU2 Cooney has completed one deployment to South Korea and one to Afghanistan. Staff Sergeant Keith Eisenschenk served nine years in the Air Force Reserves. Keith is married to Mike's granddaughter Brenda (Thayer) Eisenschenk. Yan Clermont, an officer in the Army JAG Corp (Judge Advocate General), served in Alaska and is now stationed in Germany. Yan is the husband of Mike's great-granddaughter Ashley (Thayer) Clermont.

Great-grandson Andrew Cooney developed an interest in the military at an early age; in this photo he is seen in first grade wearing Mike's military hat while his grandfathers spoke about the service. David proudly displayed Mike's World War II memorabilia on Memorial Day for his grandson's class.

Retirement Photo of Lt. Col. David Leroy Thayer, Mike and Helen's son.

Seven possible new doctors for the Fairmont area were guests of the Medical Opportunities Committee of the Chamber of Commerce. Five students of the University of Minnesota medical school are pictured with David Miller, Fairmont Chamber of Commerce president, U.B. Idstrom, hospital board, Drs. Neil Nickerson and E.A. Thayer of the hospital staff. L-R around the table are: Steve Puffer, Bill Young, Dr. Nickerson, John Beecher, U.B. Idstrom, David Miller, Bill McConahey, Dennis Nousainne, and Dr. Thayer. From *The Sentinel* photo by Bob Schroeder.

14

COMMUNITY INVOLVEMENT

Mike was a member of the Kiwanis Club and director of the Fairmont Chamber of Commerce. He was also a member of the Masonic Lodge and Osman Temple of the Shrine. He attended the Fairmont Methodist Church and was chairman of the board for the church. He was also president of the board for the Fairmont Interlaken Golf Club. He was a member of the VFW and the Lee C. Prentice American Legion Post No. 36, both in Fairmont. When he was a resident of the Methodist retirement home in Fairmont, he arranged to donate money toward a portion of the stained glass window in the chapel. He died before the window was finished, but would be happy he helped make it possible for others to enjoy its beauty.

Saturday, May 6, 1967 - 3
THE SENTINEL

Dr. Thayer Gets Citation From Radio

Dr. E.A. Thayer, Fairmont physician, is recipient of a WCCO Radio "Good Neighbor" award.

He was recognized recently on the "Good Morning" program.

The program transcript, which was sent with the award certificate, had this to say:

"Today's WCCO Radio Good Neighbor is Dr. Ellsworth A. (Mike) Thayer of Fairmont.

DR. THAYER

"He was born in Clarissa, Minn., almost 60 years ago. He attended West High School in Minneapolis, graduated from the University of Minnesota Medical School, and took his internship at St. Paul Anchor Hospital.

"Now he's in active practice at Fairmont. He has been extremely helpful to the Minnesota Academy of General Practice — as a charter member dating from 1946, as secretary-treasurer and last year's president.

"After retiring as president he became chairman of the committee on membership and credentials, working with medical students through various programs.

"Last week he was honored by the academy with the highest award—the Merit Award."

Dr. Thayer is a member of Kiwanis and a director of the Chamber of Commerce.

In 1967 Mike received the WCCO Good Neighbor Award, in part based on his activities in the medical profession, especially with the Academy of General Practice.

163

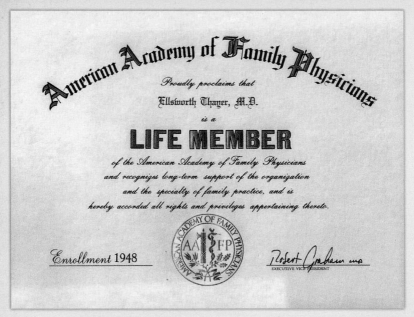

Mike also encouraged medical students to work in family practice. In 1967 he received the highest award given by the Academy of General Practice, the Merit Award.

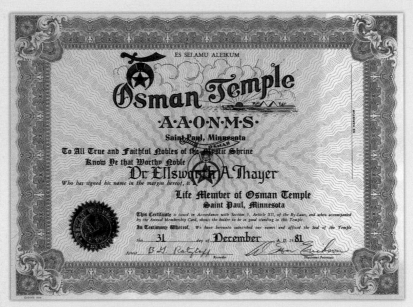

Mike received this certificate in 1990 in recognition of his 50 years as a member of the Grand Lodge of Minnesota Ancient Free and Accepted Masons. At his death he had 60 years of membership.

Legion Of Honor

Be it known that

Ellsworth Thayer

has been a Kiwanian for a period of

FiftyYears

as shown by the official organization records.

And be it further known that this member is hereby accorded
distinctive recognition
and has the admiration and gratitude of this club,
the district and Kiwanis International

Kiwanis Club Of

Fairmont

Rodney A. Lund. EC
Club President

Michael M. Lundgreen
Club Secretary

Glen M. Bagnell
President, Kiwanis International

_____
Secretary, Kiwanis International

AUGUST 31, 1999
Presented

Certificate Number 7229

Mike was a member of the Kiwanis Club from 1949 until his death in 2000. This certificate honored his 50th year of membership.

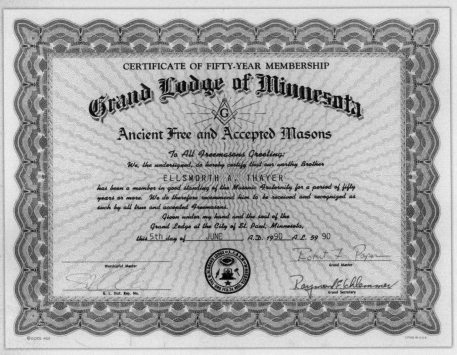

Mike was proud of the Shriners hospitals for children in the Twin Cities and all the service work the Shriners did. As a supporter of the Shriners hospitals he would buy tickets for the circus for any grandkids and great-grandchildren who lived close enough to attend. The proceeds of the circus went to the Shriner's Children's Hospital in St. Paul.

While earning your daily bread, be sure you share a slice with those less fortunate.

— *Quoted in* P.S. I Love You, *compiled by H. Jackson Brown, Jr.*

We make a living by what we get, but we make a life by what we give.

— *Winston Churchill*

What we have done for ourselves alone dies with us;
what we have done for others and the world remains and is immortal.

— *Albert Pike*

Methodists Note Year's Progress, Elect Dr. Thayer to Head Board

Methodists learned last night about the progress of their church during the past 12 months and elected officers.

Sunday school attendance climbed 11 per cent, it was reported. Value of church property passed the $200,000 mark. Membership in the Women's Society of Christian Service (WSCS) was up. Total church membership was down slightly.

Dr. E. A. Thayer, physician, was elected chairman by the official board at the annual meeting. The board is the governing body of the congregation. He succeeds Thomas Thompson.

The Sentinel, Fairmont, MN, ca 1962.

Volunteers don't get paid, not because they're worthless, but because they're priceless.

— *Sherry Anderson*

Unselfish and noble actions are the most radiant pages in the biography of souls.

— *David Thomas*

U. S. Army

SCU   1978

Greetings

Oakland Area
Station Hospital
CHRISTMAS DAY, 1943
Oakland, California

Mike attended a World War II alumni dinner in Oakland, California in 1978.
They enjoyed visiting about the war over dinner and a program. Helen went
with him to the reunion.

15

KEEPING IN TOUCH

Three doctors whom Mike met during his service became lifelong friends. Mike met Joe Wandke in California, and they were stationed together in South Carolina, Tinian, and Fukuoka. Following the war, they practiced together in Fairmont. Ray Sanford, a pathologist in Mankato, Minnesota, appeared with Mike in several photos taken on Tinian. Another lifelong friend who was with him in Tinian but with another unit was Dr. James Fitch, a veterinarian from Fairmont.

Mike's daughter Susie wrote to Bill several times from 2004 to 2008 asking about the war, and Bill responded. In a telephone conversation, he told her he remembered seeing the *Enola Gay* in the hangar but that none of them were told what it was for. Bill was escorting nurses for a tour of the Quonset huts that were being built for an invasion of Japan when the commander pointed to the "big plane." Col. Temple was the commanding officer of the 309th. Susie did not remember Mike talking about the *Enola Gay*, although he had a picture of it in his collection.

Bill also told Susie that he, Mike, and Joe explored the caves where the Japanese hid when the American forces began assaulting the island. They, along with many other GIs, attended the Saturday night youth rallies held in the auditorium of the Seinan Baptist College in Fukuoka. Bill, Mike, and some other doctors from the 309th sang in the chapel choir during the Sunday

REV. WILLIAM S. ACKERMAN
3 ST. PAUL PLACE
LAKEHURST, N.J. 08733

28 December 2001

Dear David:and Edna:

Thank you so much for your card and **enclosed** letter telling me
about your parents. Not receiving a Christmas card from them I
wrote to Mrs. Otto Wandke in Fairmont asking her to let me know
about the Thayers. As you probably know Dr. Otto Wandke was also
on the Staff of the 309th General Hospital which went overseas to
Tinian during the war in 1945. And Dr. Raymond Sanford in
Mankato, Minn. was in our Hospital.

My family and I took trips across the country in 1950, 1954 and 1956.
On two of those trips we stayed overnight with your Mother and Dad
on our way back East. I think it was the last two trips. Then in
1991 my wife, Dottie, and I stayed over night with your parents when
we were on a trip across the country. My first wife, Virginia, and
I had taken those earlier trips with our two children, David and
Peggy. Virginia died in 1989 after we had been married 52 years.

Your parents were in the East either in 1960 or 1961 to attend the
AMA Convention in Atlantic City and they stopped by to visit us
in Livingston, N. J. where I was the pastor of the Presbyterian
Church. They drove up from Atlantic City with Dr. and Mrs. Robert
Bourland from Tennessee. Bob had also been in the 309th Hospital.
So you see I have many fond memories of your Dad especially inasmuch
as we were tent mates on Tinian from July 1945 until March 1946.
He was a wonderful friend and jovial companion during those days.

I send you my belated condolences in the loss of your parents. I
cherish the memories of them and thank God for becoming acquainted
with such fine folks. Minnesota became a focal point of interest
through meeting them. You had parents of real character and
integrity.

My Son, David, is 61 and works for Macy's in New York. My daughter,
Peggy, 60, lost her husband in 1990 at age 51. She had lived in New
Jersey until last June when she moved to Athens, Penn. where her
daughter and husband live. She bought a house on the same street as
her daughter who recently gave birth to her first child. I now have
six great-granddaughters.

I retired from the Presbyterian Church of Livingston after serving
as pastor for thirty-three years. We moved to a Retirement Village,
Leisure Knoll in Lakehurst,N.J. I then served for over 15 years as
a Minister of Visitation at the Presbyterian Church of Toms River,
part-time. I"re-retired" in April 1999. Dottie will be retiring in
April after serving 10 years as a Minister of Visitation at our Toms
River Church, part-time. I celebrated my 90th birthday earlier this
month. I have been blest with health and thank God for that. We plan
to take a trip in May to Norway for three weeks. Remember me to your
sister Susie. With every good wish to you for a healthy and Happy New
Year.   Sincerely,   *Bill Ackerman*

Pastor Bill Ackerman, who was Mike's tent mate on Tinian came to visit him twice
after the war, and the two wrote letters back and forth. David sent Bill a Christmas
letter informing him of Mike's death, and Bill wrote in return to David and Edna.

worship. Several times, they visited other U.S. units that were stationed on Tinian before the Atom Bomb was released over Hiroshima. When Susie had tried to call Bill one more time, she was sad to learn that he had passed away on April 8, 2010. Susie stated it was a blessing that she had a chance to talk and correspond with one of dad's tent mates.

The Rev. William S. Ackerman
Harrogate A-191
400 Locust Street
Lakewood, NJ 08701

3 August 2007

Dear Syusie:

    At long last I am getting aroud to answering your question about some of the things your Dad and I did when on the Island of Tinian during our stay there back in 1944. My delay has been the death of my dear wife, Dottie, who died on August 10th last year. How I miss her!

    Have I written to you since that date? I moved into this Retirement facility in Lakewood, just four miles from where we lived in Leisure Knoll. There are 300 apartment here. I get my breakfast and supper in my small kitchen and eat my dinner at noon in t e large Dining Room. Did I send you my Christmas letter last year? If not, I can send you a copy.

    Please excuse thus typing as I am using a new standard machine that I recently purchased. I am in good healt and walk each day about a mile around the complex of Harrogate

    Your Dad and I and Joe Wandke used to explore the Japanese caves that they retired to when the American forces began assaulting the island. We also attended the Saturday Night Youth Rallies held in the auditorium of the Seinan Baptist College in Fukuoka. Many GIs also attended them. Your Dad and I also sang in the Chapel Choir during our Sunday worship. A few other doctors from our 309th General Hospital also sang in the Choir. On a number of occasions we visited other U. S. units who were stationed on Tinian before the Atom Bomb was realeased over Hiroshima in August. Wasn't it around the 15th of August? Memory seems to fail me with thos days of long ago. I hope these few insights will be helpful to you.

    My family are all well, thank the Lord. I now have 11 Great-grandchildren and will be driven by my son, Dav: and his wife in October out to Athens, Penn. to Baptize the 11th in the Presbyterian Church.

    How is your brother David? I have been t inkikl: of Minnesota the last two days as I saw on TV the awful collapse of that huge bridge in Minneapolis. It would be great to hear from you. Do you recall when my family on our way West one summer stayed overnight at your parents/ home in Fairmont?

    With all the best to you and your companion Jerr;

Sincerely,

Bill Ackerman

All ten of Mike's grandchildren attended his funeral. This photo of Helen and the grandchildren was taken at the reception that followed at the church. Back row, left to right: Allen Thayer, Roger Thayer, Steve Bakken, Scott Thayer; Middle row, left to right: Doug Wright, Joni Newton, Jenny Wise, Brenda Eisenschenk, Tamara Thayer; Kneeling in front next to Helen is Dr. Kim Thayer.

16

EFFECTS OF THE WAR
ON A COUNTRY DOCTOR

The question can be asked, what effect did the war have on a country doctor? Mike's story is not one of fighting in bloody battles, although he saw the horrors of war when he treated Americans and Japanese who were wounded in the atomic bombings.

Possibly the two largest sacrifices Mike made in the war were his loneliness and the interruption of his medical practice. He often wrote in his journal of his loneliness and his inability to see why he was on Tinian. That likely led him to feel closer to his family when he returned and helped provide the stimulus for many happy family gatherings. On December 10, 2000, a family Christmas celebration was held at the home of his grandson, Roger Thayer, and his wife, Joanne, in Trimont, Minnesota. The next day, Mike suffered a stroke, and he died on December 12 with family present at Fairmont Community Hospital. A funeral service celebrating Mike's life was held at the Methodist church in Fairmont, followed by military honors at the cemetery.

The second sacrifice was the interruption of the medical practice. Mike received less pay in the service than he would have received at home. Being brought up during The Depression and the effects of the war years might have made him more prudent in his handling of money. He continued to always

E.A. Thayer

FAIRMONT — Services for Dr. E.A. Thayer, 93, of Fairmont will be 11 a.m. today at the United Methodist Church, Fairmont. Burial will be in Fairview Memorial Park, Fairmont.

Thayer died Tuesday evening, Dec. 12, 2000, at Fairmont Community Hospital. Visitation was 5-7 p.m. Thursday at Lakeview Funeral Home, Fairmont, and one hour prior

to services at the church. There was a Masonic service 7 p.m. Thursday at the funeral home.

Ellsworth Albert Thayer was born June 12, 1907, in Clarissa, son of LeRoy and Maude (Cooper) Thayer. He graduated from West High School, Minneapolis, in 1925, and attended the University of Minnesota Medical School. He married Helen Gallehue on Nov. 13, 1930, in Minneapolis. He received his medical degree in 1931 and served an internship at Ancker Hospital, St. Paul. He began his medical practice in Truman, in July 1932, and started Truman Community Hospital in 1940. He closed the hospital when he entered the service. He served in the U.S. Army from 1943-46 at Oakland Regional Hospital, Oakland, Calif., in the South Pacific and Japan. After his discharge, he began a medical practice in Fairmont.

He was a member and past chairman of the board of the United Methodist Church, charter member and past president of Minnesota Academy of Family Practice, helped found the current Fairmont Medical Clinic, member of Masonic Lodge, Osman Temple of the Shrine, Lee C. Prentice American Legion Post No. 36, and member and past president of Interlaken Golf Club, Fairmont.

Survivors include: wife, Helen Thayer of Fairmont; son, David Thayer and wife, Edna, of Elysian; daughter, Suzanne Wright of Aitkin; 10 grandchildren; 24 great-grandchildren; daughter-in-law, Elaine Thayer of Park Rapids; and one niece.

He was preceded in death by his parents, one son, one brother, two sisters, one son-in-law and one brother-in-law.

REMEMBER

Remember the country doctor heading on his way
Thru a blustery blizzard on Armistice Day
He walked two miles thru wind and cold
To fix a broken bone I'm told
What a great man with a heart of gold!

Remember delivering babies was his specialty
He even delivered some grandkids, but not me
You couldn't go many places where someone wouldn't say
That Doc Thayer had helped them in some way
Perhaps that's why you're with us here today?

Remember being sick was easier for me
Because my grandpa I'd get to see
Although I wouldn't always go on my own will
Sometimes my tonsils would make me ill
Then he'd take out his pad and prescribe a pill.

Remember the love my grandparents shared
70 years shows how much they really cared
They raised 3 children, Dave, Bill and Suzi
Who had 10 children of their own you see
And 24 great-grandchildren carry on his legacy.

Remember pipe smoke that filled the air
And prickly kisses from his mustache hair
Doing puzzles or playing tidily winks
While the women did dishes by the kitchen sink
And we'd wait to open our presents, I think.

Remember from the lake, to condo, to Lakeview
We'd love to come visit for a day or two
I'll hold dear to my heart our time together last Sunday
Grandpa, thanks for the memories is what I'm trying to say
Watch over us and protect us in your heavenly way!

Poem written by granddaughter Brenda (Thayer) Eisenschenk and given as a eulogy at the funeral.

Mike's obituary from *The Sentinel*.

support his mother. His deployment imposed a financial burden on the family; boarders were taken in, and David worked at a young age. They had double expense in maintaining a home in Truman while the family rented a house first in Oakland and later in South Carolina in order to be near Mike.

Lessons Learned

Mike was always compassionate. Did the war make him even more compassionate to those who had problems or who were less fortunate? Former patients of his describe him as a very compassionate man who would listen to their problems and complaints. Dr. Thayer was known for his great sense of humor and excellent bedside manner.

Mike used opportunities during the war to learn more about medicine and farming. He worked alongside Japanese doctors and learned techniques that were not common in America. He also taught them American techniques. Out of necessity, he also learned more about performing surgeries. Because of his time in Japan working with the Japanese to heal the wounded with them, he developed a respect for the people. Mike admired their resourcefulness after the bombs had destroyed many of their supplies such as when the Japanese doctors used the strips from palm branch leaves for sutures for skin grafting. He always had an interest in farming and over the years was fortunate enough to have invested in three farms to rent out to farmers. While in Japan he was fascinated to learn some of the techniques used by their farmers.

Perhaps an abstract lesson that he learned was that we do not always know the master plan in life. He did not know that the island of Tinian provided a corridor for the air strike that eventually dropped the atomic bombs which ended the war. He thought that being on the island was such a waste of time. He questioned the wisdom of the higher officers in the service. After the war, he realized the importance of Tinian and maintaining control of an island that previous American soldiers had fought to capture. He was asked if he felt it was necessary to drop the Atomic bomb. His reply was that many more lives would have been lost if the war continued, because Japan was not about to easily surrender.

In life, he believed in a God who also had a master plan. He did not always understand why certain things happened such as the death of his son from cancer at the age of 38. But he did believe in God and trusted him to guide his ways.

After the war, the island was returned to the natives who were most appreciative as witnessed by the medal received by Dr. Thayer and others who served on the island.

The following article is from the *Elysian Enterprise*:

Our Grateful Islands Remember

In 2005, the Northern Mariana Islands, a commonwealth in political union with the United States, struck a medallion commemorating the 60th anniversary of the end of World War II. Military who served on Tinian or Saipan during World War II are

Saipan and Tinian Island medallion awarded.

eligible to receive this medallion. As part of the October 8, 2012 program of the Scott Hosier World War II Round Table in Rochester, Minnesota two veterans were given this honor and recognized in front of about three hundred people for their service.

Captain Ellsworth A. Thayer, MD US Army (deceased) was assigned to the 309th Hospital on Tinian as a field hospital surgeon. He participated in the early phase of the Japan occupation providing health care for both the military and citizens after the atomic bombings under very primitive conditions. His son, Lt. Col. David L. Thayer, Air Force, accepted his medallion on his behalf. David is from Elysian, Minnesota. Also attending the program was Ellsworth's granddaughter Tammy Thayer and his great-granddaughter Andrea Thayer both of Rochester, Minnesota.

Corporal Patrick J. Cooney, US Marine Corp, was assigned to the 2nd Armored Amphibian Battalion, attached to the 2nd and 4th Marine Divisions. He was the 75mm turret gunner on an LTV-(A)4 amphibious tank. He and his crew participated in all first wave landings on Saipan, Tinian, as well as on Iwo Jima where he was wounded and for which he received a purple heart. Patrick is from Le Center, MN. Also attending the program was his wife Vi and his daughter and son-in-law, Sheri and Rich Clymer of Hastings.

Colonel Walt Halloran was the presenting officer. He is a World War II, Korean, and Vietnam veteran with 30 years of service. He was a POW in World War II.

Left to right: Cpl. Patrick Cooney, Lt. Col. David Thayer, and Col. Walt Halloran.

First Lieutenant Ellsworth "Mike" Thayer

Afterword

Author's Portrait of a Real Hero

When I first read through all of my grandfather's letters and journal, I thought about how special it was to have a real hero for a grandfather, who put his medical career on hold to serve his country in World War II. I thought about how brave it was to go to Japan so soon after the atomic bombs had been dropped exposing him to possible unknown side effects in order to provide needed medical treatment to both civilians and military. As I researched World War II, I learned that it was full of heroes not just on the battlefield but in the actions of civilians who supported the cause.

At the monthly World War II Roundtables, I heard speakers on a wide range of topics including a Navajo code talker who had translated messages into his own language so the enemy could not break the code. I heard a woman speak who acted as a spy to deliver messages to our military in Europe and the danger she put herself through. Another had survived a kamikaze attack on a Navy ship. During the rescue so many were getting off the ship to board another ship that their weight concentrated on the one side of the ship caused the ship to tip and sink faster in that direction so the captain ordered the rescue ship to pull away leaving the crew left on board to save the ship or face certain death as they would sink. The few men left on the ship went to great lengths to get the ship upright and bail out the water as they made it to shore and survived. Heroes were also found among the Tuskegee Airmen who while experiencing discrimination served with honor, while proving in the air their equality and skill as pilots.

Many women became heroes in this war by serving their country in the WAVES, the WAC, the WAFS, the WASP, and as nurses in the Army. They also served as "human calculators," to do quick equations to help the gunnery officers on the battlefield, and by taking factory jobs to make munitions like Rosie the Riveter, and opening the first day cares to allow other women to work outside the home.

At these World War II Roundtables, I met an interesting group of veterans whose caps read "Too Young to Serve World War II Veteran." When I asked what that meant I was told that they had fibbed about their ages to enlist in the service and did get by with it. Another interesting speaker I met was a man who served in our photographer corps whose job was to photograph the war. These men often found themselves in the middle of battles without guns to protect themselves as they shot pictures to capture the history of the war.

What about the farm family of five sons who send four sons to battle while leaving the youngest at home to do the farm work of five men, while they enlisted and came home as heroes…doesn't he too deserve recognition for keeping the farm going giving them something to come home to? Also not to be forgotten are the civilians who bought war bonds, planted victory gardens, and sent care packages to our troops; didn't they support and aide in the outcome of the war? The list goes on and on of the heroes I met while researching this book about my grandfather. So I ask the question, does this make my grandfather's role in the war any less of a hero?

The answer is that I have learned this war produced many heroes. My grandfather was a hero to me in many new ways. First to face such financial troubles as a teenager during "The Great Depression," which did not stop him from achieving his goal to become a doctor. After accomplishing his dream he never forgot what it was like to struggle and he felt true compassion for his community and for those less fortunate. Isn't it a hero who helps out others and expects nothing in return? He often provided free medicine without others knowing and not wanting any recognition for it. Imagine one minute fighting Japan as an enemy and after their surrender entering their country as a new allied comrade. Some Americans returned to America after the war harboring hate for the enemy even after the war was over. Doc showed instant camaraderie when entering their country and worked beside their doctors with a common goal to heal the wounded. He was unofficially a great American ambassador by showing he wanted to understand their culture and people by taking Japanese language classes, going into the community and meeting the locals and making friends. How quickly he changed his mindset from fighting the enemy to creating new relationships once they surrendered. Who knew what the dangers might have been being exposed to the aftermath of the atomic bomb while in Fukuoka, but a hero doesn't worry about it.

Besides the war, I feel he showed heroic acts in his field of medicine always providing care despite a patient's ability to pay. He was innovative in starting the Minnesota Academy of General Practice with a group of doctors. He was very active in his community and supported community growth. He showed true devotion to his profession and compassion to his patients and the whole community. On a personal family perspective, my grandfather was a hero in how he role modeled the importance of family. He cared for his mother and supported her for the rest of her life. He was a loving and devoted husband for 70 years. We witnessed how he cherished his wife and was so respectful to her. As a father and grandfather, he was always so supportive going to our concerts, play performances, Baptisms, graduations, etc. In every aspect of his life, my grandfather was nothing short of a Real American Hero!

Timeline

June 12, 1907	Ellsworth Albert Thayer born in Clarissa, Minnesota.
1912	Henry Ford invents the assembly line to mass-produce the Model T Ford.
1918	Armistice is signed between Allied Powers and Germany in the 11th hour of the 11th day of the 11th month.
1920	Women granted the right to vote.
1921	Insulin discovered.
1925	Mike graduates from West High School in Minneapolis, Minnesota.
1925	Mike enters the University of Minnesota Medical School.
1927	The first trans-Atlantic flight by Charles Lindberg from New York to Paris takes 33 hours.
1928	Penicillin invented.
1928	Stalin gains control of Russia.
October 27, 1929	"Black Tuesday" stock market crash.
April 16, 1930	Mike's father, Leroy David, dies of a heart attack.
November 13, 1930	Mike marries Helen Gallehue in Minneapolis, Minnesota.
1931	Mike receives his medical degree and serves an internship at Ancker Hospital in St. Paul, Minnesota.
September 17, 1931	Mike and Helen's first child, David Leroy, is born.
1932	Franklin Delano Roosevelt becomes president.

July 1932	Mike begins his medical practice in Truman, Minnesota.
June 12, 1935	Mike and Helen's second son, William Roger, is born.
1940	Mike opens the Truman Community Hospital.
1941	Mike and Helen's third child, Suzanne Alana, is born.
1943	Mike enters the U.S. Army and closes the hospital.
October 27, 1943	Mike's service in the U.S. Army begins.
August 6, 1945	Atomic bomb dropped on Hiroshima.
August 9, 1945	Atomic bomb dropped on Nagasaki.
August 15, 1945	Japan sends word of surrender.
September 2, 1945	Japan signs Instrument of Surrender officially ending World War II. Known as V-J Day in the U.S. for Victory over Japan Day.
September 14, 1945	Mike and the other troops on Tinian receive word of the surrender at 9:00 a.m.
October 10, 1945	Ship arrived with orders to take Doc Thayer and others to Sasebo and Kure but he had no orders to go.
October 22, 1945	Orders clarified and they left Tinian in route to Sasebo.
October 31, 1945	Anchored outside Sasebo for a week.
November 7, 1945	Mike was brought to Fukuoka, Japan.
February 5, 1946	Left Fukuoka and traveled by train, boat, and plane to get home following the route of Tokyo, Guam, Kwajalein, Hawaii, and finally arrives home in Truman, Minnesota on April 5, 1946.